A TALE OF TV

A PLAY IN TWO ACTS

BY

BRIAN J. BURTON

BASED ON THE NOVEL
BY
CHARLES DICKENS

HANBURY PLAYS

KEEPER'S LODGE
BROUGHTON GREEN
DROITWICH
WORCESTERSHIRE WR9 7EE

BY THE SAME AUTHOR:-

ROSMERSHOLM (A new English version)
SWEENEY TODD THE BARBER
THE MURDER OF MARIA MARTEN or THE RED BARN
LADY AUDLEY'S SECRET or DEATH IN LIME TREE WALK
THE DRUNKARD or DOWN WITH DEMON DRINK!
THREE HISSES FOR VILLAINY!!!
CHEERS, TEARS AND SCREAMERS!
EAST LYNNE or NEVER CALLED ME MOTHER!
BEING OF SOUND MIND
MURDER PLAY
DRINK TO ME ONLY
THE LAST LAUGH
FROM THREE TO FOUR
HE AND SHE
DEATH MASQUE
FACE THE QUEEN
A QUESTION OF PROFIT
TEA WITH JASON
GHOST OF A CHANCE
SUDDEN DEATH
FOILED AGAIN!
VISITING TIME
NINE WOMEN - NO MEN
LINES OF COMMUNICATION (15 ONE-ACT PLAYS)
THE WOODPILE
A BEAR WITH A SORE HEAD (adapted from Chekhov)

First published 1989

© Brian J. Burton 1989

ISBN:- 185205 078 0

CHARACTERS

in order of appearance

THE VOICE OF THE NARRATOR
A WAITER
JARVIS LORRY
LUCIE MANETTE
MISS PROSS
JACQUES 1
ERNEST DEFARGE
DOCTOR MANETTE
JERRY CRUNCHER
MRS CRUNCHER
A BANK CLERK
COURT USHER
THE SOLICITOR GENERAL
JOHN BARSAD
MR STRYVER
A JUDGE
ROGER CLY
THOMAS KEMP
CHARLES DARNAY
SYDNEY CARTON
A CUSTOMER
A SECOND CUSTOMER
A MAN
GASPARD
A CHILD
THE MARQUIS DE ST EVREMONDE
MADAME DEFARGE
SELBY
GABELLE
A ROADMENDER
A TURNKEY
AN OFFICER
USHER AT THE TRIBUNAL
THE PRESIDENT OF THE TRIBUNAL
THE FOREMAN OF THE JURY
1st SOLDIER
A GAOLER
A SEAMSTRESS
A MAN BY THE GUILLOTINE
1st WOMAN
2nd WOMAN
3rd WOMAN
MEMBERS OF THE CROWD

IT IS POSSIBLE TO PRESENT THE PLAY
WITH A CAST OF 20 PLUS THE CROWD

SCENES

ACT ONE

Scene One	The breakfast room of the George Hotel in Dover 1775
Scene Two	The wine shop of Ernest Defarge in Paris A few days later
Scene Three	A garret above the wine shop. A few minutes later
Scene Four	Jerry Cruncher's lodgings in Whitefriars. 5 years later
Scene Five	A courtroom at the Old Bailey. The same day
Scene Six	The dining room of a tavern. Later the same evening
Scene Seven	The wine shop in Paris. A few weeks later
Scene Eight	A room in the chateau of the Marquis. Later the same day
Scene Nine	Doctor Manette's house in Soho. A year later
Scene Ten	The same. An evening in August
Scene Eleven	Jerry Cruncher's lodgings. Later the same year
Scene Twelve	The wine shop in Paris. A few weeks later

ACT TWO

Scene One	The garden of Doctor Manette's house. Later that year
Scene Two	Doctor Manette's house. The following morning. and over a period of years in London and Paris
Scene Three	Jarvis's office in Tellson's Bank. 3 months later
Scene Four	A guard room in Paris. 2 days later
Scene Five	A room in Tellson's Bank in Paris. A few days later
Scene Six	The Manettes' lodgings in Paris. 15 months later
Scene Seven	A tribunal in Paris. Several months later
Scene Eight	A room in Tellson's Bank in Paris. The same day
Scene Nine	A prison cell. The next day
Scene Ten	The Manettes' lodgings in Paris. A few minutes later
Scene Eleven	At the guillotine. Shortly afterwards

THE PRODUCTION GIVEN BY THE CRESCENT THEATRE AT WARWICK CASTLE WAS 'PROMENADE THEATRE' WITH THE VARIOUS SCENES SET IN A NUMBER OF LOCATIONS THROUGHOUT THE COURTYARD THERE WAS NO SCENERY APART FROM THE BACKDROP OF THE CASTLE ITSELF. BUT THIS PLAY HAS BEEN WRITTEN SO THAT IT CAN BE PRESENTED IN ANY THEATRICAL FORM - IN THE ROUND - THRUST STAGE OR TRADITIONAL PROSCENIUM.

This dramatization of A TALE OF TWO CITIES was first presented in the courtyard of WARWICK CASTLE by THE CRESCENT THEATRE COMPANY on July 8th 1989 with the following cast:-

DOCTOR MANETTE — ARTHUR DUDLESTON
SYDNEY CARTON — MICHAEL BARRY
CHARLES DARNAY — MIKE VENABLES
JARVIS LORRY — GUY RADFORTH
DEFARGE — IAN THOMPSON
JERRY CRUNCHER — NOËL ALEXANDER
BARSAD — BRIAN WILSON
LUCIE MANETTE — BRIDGET MILNE
MISS PROSS — SHEILA BERRY
MADAME DEFARGE — MARY DAVIS
JUDGE — FRANK JONES
A CHILD — LUCY WALLIS
SOLICITOR GENERAL, GASPARD, OFFICER, PROSECUTOR — ANDREW COWIE
STRYVER, MARQUIS, PRESIDENT OF THE TRIBUNAL — IAN HUDSON
JACQUES 1, BANK CLERK, TURNKEY, GAOLER — JASON DODD
MRS CRUNCHER, A CUSTOMER, A SEAMSTRESS — NICOLA BROTHWELL
WAITER, SELBY, USHER — PHILIP EDMUNDSON
ROGER CLY, A ROADMAN, 1st SOLDIER — BEN WATKINS
THOMAS KEMP, MAN IN CROWD, JURY FOREMAN — ALAN CROCKETT
USHER, GABELLE — STEWART SNAPE
1st WOMAN, 2nd CUSTOMER — JANET CROCKETT
WOMEN — JENNET MARSHALL, PAULINE RATTIGAN
DRUMMER — DAVE HENNESSEY
VOICE OF THE NARRATOR — BRIAN J. BURTON
CROWD — ELIZABETH FREETH, ROSEMARY GOWERS, SARAH WALLIS, JOHN COLVIN, BILL GRANT, KEITH MACHIN, CHESSMAN SAUNDERS and members of the cast listed above.

DIRECTED by RON BARBER

COSUME DESIGN..BRENDA BEASLEY   MOB DIRECTOR..DAVID HANKIN
LIGHTING DESIGN.. PAUL COOPER   SOUND DESIGN..KEN CLARKE
STAGE MANAGERS..DAVID GRIFFITHS and MIKE LACEY
PROPERTIES..PENNY VENABLES and SHEILA BULL
GUILLOTINE designed by JOHN BAILEY
and CONSTRUCTED by PHILIP PARSONS
FURNITURE by THE ROYAL SHAKESPEARE COMPANY
COSTUMES supplied by THE CRESCENT THEATRE WARDROBE

TO

RON and BRENDA

and

THE 'TWO CITIES' COMPANY

VOICE OF THE NARRATOR

It was the best of times. It was the worst of times. It was the age of wisdom. It was the age of foolishness. It was the epoch of belief. It was the epoch of incredulity. It was the season of light. It was the season of darkness. It was the Spring of hope. It was the Winter of despair.

It was the year of Our Lord - one thousand, seven hundred and seventy five.

ACT ONE

Scene One

THE BREAKFAST ROOM OF THE GEORGE HOTEL IN DOVER.. JARVIS LORRY, A MAN OF SIXTY, DRESSED IN BROWN IS FINISHING HIS BREAKFAST. A WAITER IS STANDING BY HIS SIDE.

JARVIS   A most excellent breakfast and much appreciated after that long coach journey from London.

WAITER   Glad to have been of service, sir.

JARVIS   Now then - a young lady should be arriving at any moment. She may ask for me as Mr Jarvis Lorry or perhaps only as the gentleman from Tellson's Bank. Would you please let me know when she arrives?

WAITER   Yes, sir. Would that be Tellson's Bank in London, sir?

JARVIS   The very same.

WAITER   We often have the honour of entertaining your gentlemen when they are travelling between London and Paris, sir.

JARVIS   We are quite a French house as well as an English one.

WAITER   Not much in the habit of travelling yourself, sir?

JARVIS   Not recently. It must be fifteen years since I was in Paris.

WAITER   I did hear a coach arrive a minute or two ago, sir. That could be the one with your lady. If you'll excuse me, sir, I'll go and find out. (EXIT)

JARVIS   (TO HIMSELF) How surprised Jerry Cruncher was when he stopped our coach on the top of Shooter's Hill to tell me to wait here in Dover for Miss Manette. I shall never forget the look on his face when I gave him the return message - 'Recalled to Life'. What was it he called it? - 'A blazing strange answer'.

WAITER   (RETURNING) Miss Manette has arrived, sir, and is most anxious to see the gentleman from Tellson's Bank.

JARVIS   Please ask her to join me here. She must be in dire need of refreshment after her journey.

WAITER   At once, sir. (CALLING THROUGH DOORWAY) If you would be kind enough to step this way.

LUCIE MANETTE ENTERS. SHE IS SEVENTEEN - A SLIGHT GIRL WITH BLONDE HAIR. SHE CARRIES A STRAW TRAVELLING HAT BY THE RIBBON. SHE IS ACCOMPANIED BY MISS PROSS - A RATHER WILD-LOOKING MIDDLE-AGED WOMAN WEARING A LARGE BONNET.

7

JARVIS	(RISING) A good day to you, ladies. I trust that you are in good health. Can I offer you some refreshment?
LUCIE	That is most kind, sir, but we have taken refreshment on the road.
JARVIS	Very well, Miss Manette. Perhaps you will allow me to introduce myself. I am Jarvis Lorry of Tellson's Bank.
LUCIE	Mr Lorry. And this is my very dear friend and companion, Miss Pross.
JARVIS	I am honoured, Miss Pross. Now, shall we sit down? (THEY DO SO) Now, Miss Manette, please tell me how much you know of the matter in hand.
LUCIE	Yesterday, I received a letter from the bank. It referred to some discovery that has been made in respect of the property of my late father who died many years ago and whom I never saw. .It would appear that it is necessary for me to travel to Paris to speak to a gentleman from the bank who is going there to meet me for that purpose.
JARVIS	Myself, Miss Manette.
LUCIE	I informed the bank that I would be most grateful if I might travel with this gentleman under his protection. I understand that a messenger was sent to you to ask you to wait here for me.
JARVIS	That is indeed so, Miss Manette, and I am honoured to be entrusted with the charge.
LUCIE	That is most kind, Mr Jarvis. The bank told me that you would supply me with full details of the matter about which they wrote to me and that I must prepare myself to finding them of a somewhat surprising nature.
JARVIS	That is so.
LUCIE	Tell me, Mr Lorry, now that we have met here in Dover, will it still be necessary for me to travel to Paris? Could you not supply me with the details here?
JARVIS	Indeed I can supply you with those details without further delay, but when I have done so, you will understand why you must accompany me to Paris.
LUCIE	Very well, Mr Lorry. Then, pray proceed. I am most anxious to hear what you have to tell me.
JARVIS	Well, Miss Manette ... (ADJUSTS HIS WIG) I ... I ... It is very difficult to know where to begin.
MISS PROSS	May I suggest the beginning, Mr Lorry?
JARVIS	Yes - thank you. Well, perhaps I might tell you the story of one of our customers - a French gentleman of great learning - a doctor like your father. He was a gentleman of considerable repute in Paris. I had the honour of knowing him there. I had been working in our Paris house for twenty years or so. That would be - let me see - oh, almost twenty years ago. This doctor married an English lady. His affairs were all in the hands of Tellson's, and I was one of the trustees.
LUCIE	But this is my father's story and, I do believe that, when

8

	I became an orphan after my mother died less than two years after my poor father, that it was you, Mr Lorry, who brought me to England. Am I not right?
JARVIS	(KISSING HER HAND) Yes, Miss Manette - it was I. You have been the ward of Tellson's ever since. Now - as you say, so far this could have been the story of your late father but here is the difference. Just suppose that your father had not died - suppose that he had just disappeared.
LUCIE	(GRASPING HIS WRIST) Disappeared? What do you mean?
JARVIS	Disappeared to some dreadful place. Then the history of your father would have been this doctor's history.
LUCIE	What dreadful place, Mr Lorry? Tell me the truth, I beg.
JARVIS	Very well. Your father has been found. He is alive.
LUCIE	Alive?
JARVIS	Yes, but just released from prison. He has been taken to the house of an old servant in Paris - a Monsieur Defarge. We are going there to identify your father and - if possible - to bring him back with us for rest and comfort after all he has endured.
LUCIE	What have they done to him? Why was he put in prison?
JARVIS	It would be far too dangerous to make any enquiries. Even I, an Englishman and a trusted servant of the bank, have to avoid direct mention of the matter. This is a secret mission. All memoranda concerning the matter are labelled and referred to by the phrase 'Recalled to Life' You see, Miss Manette, when ... What is the matter, Miss Manette? You are not listening to me.

LUCIE HAS SLUMPED ACROSS THE TABLE. MISS PROSS RISES AND PUTS HER ARMS AROUND LUCIE.

MISS PROSS	My precious - my Ladybird - there, there. (ROUNDING ON JASPER) Couldn't you tell her without frightening her to death? Do you call that being a banker?
JASPER	She will soon recover in your hands, Miss Pross, I am sure. You will be coming with us to France?
MISS PROSS	A likely thing indeed! If it was ever intended that I should go across salt water, why do you suppose Providence would have cast my lot in an island? Well, man - don't just stand there - go and fetch smelling salts, cold water and vinegar and be quick about it.
JARVIS	I'll see what I can do, Miss Pross. (HURRIED EXIT)
MISS PROSS	Pshah! (TO LUCIE) My Ladybird, my dear Ladybird.

ACT ONE

Scene Two

THE WINE SHOP OF ERNEST DEFARGE IN PARIS - A FEW DAYS LATER. MADAME DEFARGE, A DARK-HAIRED WOMAN IN HER THIRTIES, IS SEATED BEHIND THE BAR, KNITTING. CUSTOMERS

ARE SEATED AT THE TABLES. THEY ARE PLAYING CARDS AND DOMINOES. JACQUES ONE IS SEATED AT A TABLE NEAR THE BAR. THERE IS THE NOISE OF AN EXCITED CROWD OFFSTAGE. MONSIEUR DEFARGE ENTERS. HE IS A MARTIAL-LOOKING MAN IN HIS THIRTIES.

JACQUES 1   How goes it out there? Is all the spilt wine swallowed?

DEFARGE   To the last drop. Men, women and children - they all scooped it up from the cobbles. Some women dipped their headscarves into the wine and squeezed it into the mouths of their little ones. They even sucked the splinters of the broken cask.

JACQUES 1   Many of the miserable creatures barely know the taste of wine these days - or anything but black bread and death. A bitter taste they always have in their mouths and hard lives they live.

DEFARGE   Indeed it is so, Jacques. Just now, our friend Gaspard dipped his finger into the spilt wine and wrote the word 'blood' on the wall outside the shop. I told him that it was not wise to write such things in public places. He just shrugged his shoulders and walked away without saying a word. I wiped off the word 'blood' with some mud out of the gutter. It is not yet the time or the place.

JACQUES 1   Not yet, no - not yet.

JARVIS AND LUCIE ENTER. LUCIE STAYS BY THE DOOR. JARVIS CROSSES TO DEFARGE.

JARVIS   Monsieur Defarge, may I have a word with you?

DEFARGE   What can I do for you, monsieur?

JARVIS   My name is Jarvis Lorry of Tellson's Bank. I have come from London with that young lady. She is the daughter of the gentleman in your care - Doctor Manette, your old master. We are come to take him away to England.

DEFARGE   To England! Yes, I understand. Call the young lady and we will go and see him at once.

JARVIS   Thank you, Monsieur Defarge. (CALLING) Miss Manette, all is arranged. If you would come with us.

LUCIE CROSSES TO THEM.

DEFARGE   He is in a room upstairs. We will have to go out into the courtyard.

JARVIS   Is he alone?

DEFARGE   Always - of necessity.

JARVIS   Is he greatly changed?

DEFARGE   Changed? You will see. You will see. Wait a moment while I get the key to his room. (MADAME DEFARGE HANDS THE KEY TO HIM)

JARVIS   Is the door locked then? Why is that necessary?

DEFARGE   He has lived so long locked up like that, if he were not, he would be frightened - might even tear himself to pieces.

10

JARVIS	It seems hardly possible.
DEFARGE	(BITTERLY) Oh, it's possible all right. A beautiful world we live in, don't we, when such things are possible. Long live the devil! Shall we go up?
LUCIE	Mr Lorry - I fear the moment of our meeting.
JARVIS	Courage, Miss Manette - courage. The worst will soon be over. Come take my arm.

ACT ONE

Scene Three

A GARRET ABOVE THE WINE SHOP - A FEW MINUTES LATER. DOCTOR MANETTE IS SEATED ON A BENCH BY A SMALL WORK-TABLE, MAKING A SHOE.

DEFARGE	(CROSSING TO MANETTE) Good day, monsieur.
MANETTE	(WITHOUT LOOKING UP) Good day.
DEFARGE	You are still hard at work, I see.
MANETTE	(AFTER A PAUSE) Yes - I am working.
DEFARGE	You have a visitor, monsieur. Why don't you tell him what kind of shoe it is and the name of the maker?
MANETTE	My name? It is one hundred and five, North Tower. (HE RETURNS TO THE SHOEMAKING)
JARVIS	You are not a shoemaker by trade, I understand.
MANETTE	(LOOKING UP AGAIN) No - no, I taught myself here.
JARVIS	Doctor Manette, don't you remember me at all? (DOCTOR MANETTE DROPS THE SHOE ON THE FLOOR) Look at me, Doctor Manette. Do you remember nothing of an old banker friend? Isn't there something about me that you can remember?

MANETTE STARES AT HIM FOR A SHORT TIME AND THEN BENDS DOWN AND PICKS UP THE SHOE AND CONTINUES WORKING.

DEFARGE	Would you have recognised him, monsieur?
JARVIS	Hardly. There is little left of that face I knew so well.

LUCIE MOVES TOWARDS THE BENCH. DEFARGE AND JARVIS DROP BACK SLIGHTLY TO LEAVE LUCIE ALONE WITH HER FATHER.

MANETTE	(SENSING THAT SOMEONE IS CLOSE TO HIM) Who are you? (LOOKS UP AND, AFTER A PAUSE) You are not the gaoler's daughter.
LUCIE	(WITH A SIGH) No, I am not.
MANETTE	Then, who are you?

LUCIE SITS ON THE BENCH BESIDE MANETTE AND PUTS HER HAND ON HIS ARM. HE LAYS DOWN HIS KNIFE VERY SLOWLY AND LOOKS AT HER. SLOWLY, HE REMOVES A BLACKENED STRING, WITH A RAG TIED TO IT, FROM AROUND HIS NECK. HE UNFOLDS THE RAG ON HIS KNEE WITH GREAT CARE. HE THEN HOLDS UP SOME OF THE GOLDEN HAIR BEFORE SPEAKING.

11

MANETTE	It is the same. How can that be? (LOOKS AT LUCIE AND THEN, WITH GREAT DIFFICULTY) Was it you? (TOUCHES HER HAIR AND THEN LOOKS AGAIN AT THE STRANDS AND SHAKES HIS HEAD) No - no, you are too young. It cannot be. (REFOLDS RAG) What is your name, gentle angel?
LUCIE	(ON HER KNEES - GRASPING MANETTE'S HANDS) Not now - not now. I cannot tell you yet. Oh, my dear - all your agony is over. I have come to take you from it. We are going to England where you will find peace and rest at last.
JARVIS	(STEPPING FORWARD) Pardon me, Miss Manette, do you think the good doctor is fit to undertake the journey so soon?
LUCIE	Fitter than for remaining in this city, I think.
DEFARGE	She is quire right, monsieur. Doctor Manette is better out of France.
JARVIS	Very well. I'll order a carriage and post horses. Come, Miss Manette, shall we start the journey?
LUCIE	(RISING AND TAKING MANETTE'S ARM) I will bring him.
MANETTE	My tools.
DEFARGE	He wants to bring his tools, monsieur. They have been his whole life for eighteen years.
JARVIS	(GOING TO BENCH FOR THE TOOLS) I will bring them. You lead the way with your lantern.
DEFARGE	(MOVING TO EXIT) Very well, monsieur.
JARVIS	(MOVING TO EXIT AND TURNING BACK TO SPEAK TO MANETTE) Well, Doctor Manette, I hope and trust that you care to be recalled to life.
MANETTE	Recalled to life? I cannot say, monsieur. I cannot say.

ACT ONE

Scene Four

JERRY CRUNCHER'S LODGINGS IN WHITEFRIARS, FIVE YEARS LATER AND AFTERWARDS OUTSIDE TELLSON'S BANK BY TEMPLE BAR SHORTLY AFTERWARDS. JERRY CRUNCHER, AN ODD-JOB MAN, IS STANDING STRETCHING HIMSELF. HIS WIFE IS ON HER KNEES PRAYING.

JERRY	Well - here we are then - another day. Half-past eight of the clock on a March morning in the year, Anna: Dominoes Seventeen hundred and eighty. (SEES MRS CRUNCHER) Bust me if she ain't at it again! (SHE RISES) You at it again, are you? (THROWS A BOOT AT HER WHICH MISSES)
MRS C.	I was only saying my prayers.
JERRY	Saying your prayers? What do you mean by flopping yourself down and praying agin me?
MRS C.	I was not praying against you. I was praying for you.

12

JERRY	Praying for me, was you? I won't be took liberty with, I won't. Anyhow, you conceited female, what do you consider the worth of <u>your</u> prayers may be?
MRS C.	They come from the heart.
JERRY	From your heart? They ain't worth much then,
MRS C.	May God bless you and forgive you, Jerry Cruncher.
JERRY	Aggerawayter! Are you at it again?
MRS C.	I was merely asking a blessing.
JERRY	Well, don't. I ain't going to be blessed out out of house and home! Now, I must be at my trade by a quarter afore nine o'clock. I must be on my stool outside Tellson's Bank to touch my cap to the gentlemen as they go into the bank in case any of 'em is wishing to avail themselves of my services as a messenger. (HE CROSSES TO A STOOL SET LEFT, RE-POSITIONS IT SEVERAL TIMES BEFORE HE IS SATISFIED AND THEN SITS) Praying, was she? I won't have it, I say. It ain't natural, it ain't.
CLERK	(COMING OUT OF THE BANK) Messenger wanted!
JERRY	(STANDING) Yes, sir - here, sir. At your service, sir. At once, sir.
CLERK	Do you know the Old Bailey?
JERRY	Yes, sir. I know the Old Bailey all right.
CLERK	And you know our Mr Lorry?
JERRY	Better than I know the Old Bailey, sir. Or should I say, sir, better than an honest tradesman like me wishes to know the Old Bailey - if you gets my meaning, sir.
CLERK	Very well. Now, find the door where the witnesses go in and you'll be let into the court. You are to pass this note to Mr Lorry and then attract his attention so that he'll know where you are sitting. You are to remain there until Mr Lorry wants you. He needs to have a messenger at hand. Do you understand?
JERRY	Oh, yes - I understands. (WITH A CONFIDENTIAL AIR) I suppose it's forgeries they'll be trying this morning.
CLERK	Treason.
JERRY	Coo! That's quartering. That barbarous, that is.
CLERK	It is the law. Always speak well of the law.
JERRY	Oh, yes, sir - I does, sir, always, sir - always speaks well of the law, I does.
CLERK	Good. Now, here is the letter - get along now.
JERRY	Very well, sir - much obliged to you, sir.

ACT ONE

Scene Five

A COURTROOM AT THE OLD BAILEY - THE SAME DAY. THERE ARE BENCHES ON EITHER SIDE WITH MEMBERS OF THE PUBLIC, A WITNESS BOX, A DOCK, JUDGE'S BENCH, A JURY BOX ETC. JERRY RUSHES IN AND PUSHES HIS WAY THROUGH THE CROWD OF ONLOOKERS AND SITS ON A BENCH.

13

JERRY	(TO A MAN NEXT TO HIM) What's coming on next?
MAN	The treason case.
JERRY	Quartering, eh?
MAN	That's it. He's drawn on a hurdle to be half-hanged and then he's taken down and sliced open before his own face and his inside's taken out and burned while he looks on. Then his head's cut off and he's cut into quarters.
JERRY	That's if he's found guilty.
MAN	Oh, they'll find him guilty all right. No doubt about that.

THE COUNSELS ENTER AND SIT AT THEIR RESPECTIVE TABLES. JARVIS SITS WITH THE DEFENDING COUNSEL, MR STRYVER.

JERRY	(RISING) There's my man! (COUGHS LOUDLY AND WAVES THE NOTE.)

JARVIS SEES JERRY, RISES AND NODS AND SITS AGAIN. THE NOTE IS PASSED FROM HAND TO HAND WITH MUCH WHISPERING UNTIL IT REACHES JARVIS.

MAN	What's he got to do with the case?
JERRY	Blessed if I know.
MAN	What have you got to do with it then?
JERRY	Blessed if I know that either.

THE JUDGE ENTERS. ALL STAND. TWO GAOLERS BRING IN CHARLES DARNAY AND PUT HIM IN THE DOCK. THE JUDGE SITS. ALL SIT.

USHER	Silence in court! Charles Darnay, having, yesterday, pleaded not guilty to the indictment, stands before you now, charged with being a false traitor by reason that he has, on many occasions, assisted the French king, Louis, in his war against our Lord King, by coming and going between the dominions and those of the said French Louis and wickedly revealing to the said Louis what forces our illustrious Lord the King had in preparation to send to North America.
JERRY	(POINTING TO MANETTE AND LUCIE WHO ARE SEATED ON A BENCH) Who are they?
MAN	Witnesses.

SOLICITOR GENERAL (RISING TO PUT HIS CASE) My Lord, gentlemen of the jury, I appear before you on behalf of the Crown. The prisoner you see before you, though young in years, is old in his treasonable practices which claim the forfeit of his life. For many years past, the prisoner has been in the habit of passing and re-passing between France and England on secret business of which he can give no honest account. However, a noble patriot has ferreted out the nature of the prisoner's scheme and has reported his findings to the authorities. Furthermore, another patriot, the prisoner's servant, has examined his master's desk and pockets and secreted his papers. The evidence of these

14

	witnesses, together with these documents (HOLDS UP PAPERS) will provide indisputable evidence that the prisoner has furnished our enemy with lists of His Majesty's Forces. Although the lists cannot be proved to be in the prisoner's handwriting, this will be better for the prosecution as it will show the prisoner to be artful in his precautions. Therefore, gentlemen of the jury, it is your duty to find the prisoner guilty, whether you like it or not, and make an end of him.
USHER	Call the first witness - John Barsad. Call John Barsad.

BARSAD ENTERS AND GOES INTO THE WITNESS BOX.

SOLICITOR GENERAL	(COMMENCING HIS EXAMINATION) Is your name John Barsad?
BARSAD	It is.
SOL. GEN.	Now, Mr Barsad, would you be kind enough to tell the court of your former relationship with the prisoner?
BARSAD	He was a close personal friend, sir.
SOL. GEN.	Does that not make it difficult for you to give evidence against this prisoner?
BARSAD	Indeed, yes, sir. But I have resolved to sacrifice that friendship on the altar of my country.
SOL. GEN.	And why is that, Mr Barsad?
BARSAD	From the very moment that I detected his infamy, I decided that I could, no longer, cherish such a traitor.
SOL. GEN.	That is very commendable, Mr Barsad. Now, will you tell the court, in your own words, how it was that you first suspected the prisoner of treasonable activities?
BARSAD	Well, sir - I saw the prisoner, with my own eyes, passing secret government information which details our military strength.
SOL. GEN.	Will you tell the court to whom you saw this vital information being passed?
BARSAD	To enemy agents, sir. To spies.
SOL. GEN.	Now, Mr Barsad, are you in any doubt whatsoever that it was, in fact, the prisoner that you saw passing this information?
BARSAD	No, sir - I am quite certain that it was the prisoner.
SOL. GEN.	Good, good. Now, Mr Barsad, would you extend your loyal and patriotic act even further by telling the court in greater detail of the events that culminated in your discovery of this treason. In your own time, Mr Barsad. We have all the time in the world.
BARSAD	The first occasion was a night in March several years ago. The packet boat was about to sail from Calais to Dover, when the prisoner came aboard. A few minutes later he was joined by two gentlemen.
SOL. GEN.	Can you describe these gentlemen, Mr Barsad?
BARSAD	They were both of slightly less than average height and dressed in long coats and muffled against the weather.

SOL. GEN.	Did you overhear their conversation?
BARSAD	No - not exactly, sir. They whispered like conspirators.
SOL. GEN.	Could you tell what language they spoke in?
BARSAD	Oh, yes, sir - French, there was no doubt about that at all.
SOL. GEN.	And what happened next?
BARSAD	After they had been whispering together for a short while, the prisoner produced a document from the breast pocket of his overcoat and passed it to one of the men.
SOL. GEN.	I see. And did these Frenchmen remain on the vessel?
BARSAD	No, sir. They left shortly before the vessel sailed for Dover.
SOL. GEN.	And you witnessed similar encounters on other occasions?
BARSAD	Yes, sir. Once on a packet out of Calais and on another out of Boulogne.
SOL. GEN.	Those are all my questions, Mr Barsad, but before you step down, I would like to commend you for the high patriotic duty you have shown by sacrificing your personal feelings in order to identify this most wretched of men.
BARSAD	It was my duty to my country and to His Majesty, sir.
SOL. GEN.	Well spoken, Mr Barsad - well spoken. (TO THE JUDGE) I have no more questions to put to this witness, my Lord.
STRYVER	(RISING) My Lord, just a few questions, if I may be permitted to ask them on behalf of the prisoner.
JUDGE	Very well, Mr Stryver, you may proceed.
STRYVER	Mr Barsad - have you ever been a spy yourself?
BARSAD	Most certainly not.
STRYVER	What do you live on?
BARSAD	My property.
STRYVER	What is that property?
BARSAD	That does not concern this court.
STRYVER	Indeed? Allow me to be the judge of that, Mr Barsad. But I will not press the matter. Tell me, have you ever been in prison?
BARSAD	Certainly not.
STRYVER	Never in a debtors' prison?
BARSAD	I fail to see what bearing that has on the present case.
STRYVER	Indeed? Once more, allow me to decide upon that point. I ask you again - have you ever been in a debtors' prison?
BARSAD	Well, yes - but only two or three times.
STRYVER	Not five or six?
BARSAD	Perhaps. I can't remember.
STRYVER	What is your profession?
BARSAD	Gentleman.
STRYVER	Have you ever been kicked downstairs for cheating at dice?
BARSAD	That was said by the intoxicated liar who carried out the insult.
STRYVER	Have you ever lived by cheating at play?
BARSAD	Never.
STRYVER	Did you ever borrow money from the prisoner?
BARSAD	Yes.
STRYVER	Did you ever repay the money?

BARSAD	I believe not.
STRYVER	Did you or did you not borrow money from the prisoner and fail to return it? You only have to answer yes or no, Mr Barsad.
BARSAD	Very well then - yes.
STRYVER	Far from being an intimate friend of the prisoner, is it not a fact that you only know him slightly from meeting him in coaching inns and on packets?
BARSAD	I know him well.
STRYVER	And you are quite certain that you saw him with those lists?
BARSAD	Quite certain.
STRYVER	Is it not a fact that you procured those lists yourself?
BARSAD	That is a lie!
STRYVER	Do you expect to be paid for giving this evidence?
BARSAD	Certainly not.
STRYVER	But is it not a fact that you are a regular government spy and employed to lay traps?
BARSAD	That is a preposterous suggestion.
STRYVER	Answer my question, Mr Barsad - are you or are you not?
BARSAD	I am not. My motives are motives of patrotism.
STRYVER	I have no more questions, Mr Barsad. You may step down.

BARSAD LEAVES THE WITNESS BOX.

SOL. GEN.	I call my next witness - Roger Cly.
USHER	Call Roger Cly - Roger Cly.

CLY ENTERS AND GOES INTO THE WITNESS BOX.

SOL. GEN.	Is your name Roger Cly?
CLY	It is, sir - yes, sir.
SOL. GEN.	Were you in the employ of the prisoner?
CLY	Yes, sir, I was, sir - yes, sir.
SOL. GEN.	For how long, Mr Cly?
CLY	Four years, sir - yes, four years it would be, sir.
SOL. GEN.	How came you to obtain employment with the prisoner?
CLY	I met him aboard the Calais packet and I was so bold as to ask him if he wanted a handy fellow, sir. He engaged me there and then.
SOL. GEN.	When did you begin to suspect the prisoner?
CLY	Very soon after he employed me, sir. That is why I decided to keep an eye on him.
SOL. GEN.	You decided to keep an eye on him. Perhaps you would tell the court what you found when you were keeping an eye on the prisoner?
CLY	Well, sir - when I was arranging his clothes while travelling, I saw those lists in his pocket on a number of occasions.
SOL. GEN.	Did you ever see the prisoner hand these lists to another person?
CLY	Yes, sir - to French gentlemen both at Calais and Dover.
SOL. GEN.	And why did you decide to inform the authorities, Mr Cly?

17

CLY	Because I love my country, sir.
SOL. GEN.	Most praiseworthy, Mr Cly. I have no more questions.
STRYVER	Just a few points I would like to clear up, my Lord.
JUDGE	Proceed, Mr Stryver.
STRYVER	Mr Cly, did you put those lists into the prisoner's pockets?
CLY	Indeed, not, sir - no, sir. Why ever should I do a thing like that, sir?
STRYVER	You tell me, Mr Cly.
CLY	It's a lie, sir, a terrible lie. I'm honest, I am, sir - honest.
STRYVER	In that case, honest Mr Cly, perhaps you would tell the court why you were suspected of stealing a solid silver teapot?
CLY	It's a wicked lie, sir.
STRYVER	And what about a similar charge concerning a silver mustard pot?
CLY	That was silver plate, sir.
STRYVER	Was it indeed. I am most obliged to you, Mr Cly, for correcting me on that point. Now - do you know the previous witness, Mr Barsad?
CLY	Very slightly, sir - only very slightly.
STRYVER	And for how long have you know him only very slightly?
CLY	Seven or eight years.
STRYVER	Seven or eight years.
CLY	But it's only a coincidence that we are both here today, sir.
STRYVER	And is it also a coincidence that Mr Barsad's motive for informing the authorities was also one of patriotism?
CLY	I am a true Briton, sir - a true Briton.
STRYVER	I am sure, Mr Cly - I am sure. No more questions.
SOL. GEN.	(AS CLY LEAVES THE BOX) Call the next witness - Mr Jarvis Lorry.

JARVIS GOES INTO THE BOX.

SOL. GEN.	Mr Lorry - are you a clerk in Tellson's Bank?
JARVIS	I am.
SOL. GEN.	On a certain Friday night in November, five years ago, did business occasion you to travel between London and Dover on the Mail?
JARVIS	It did.
SOL. GEN.	Were there other passengers on the Mail?
JARVIS	Two.
SOL. GEN.	And did they alight on the road in the course of the night?
JARVIS	They did.
SOL. GEN.	Now, Mr Lorry - look upon the prisoner. Was he one of those two passengers?
JARVIS	They were both wrapped up and the night was dark.
SOL. GEN.	So the prisoner may have been one of them?
JARVIS	That is possible - yes.
SOL. GEN.	Have you ever seen the prisoner before?
JARVIS	Yes, I was returning from France a few days later and he came aboard the packet at Calais and sailed to Dover.

SOL. GEN.	Were you travelling alone, Mr Lorry?
JARVIS	No. I was with a lady and gentleman who are in the Court.
SOL. GEN.	That will be all, Mr Lorry. You may step down.

JARVIS LEAVES THE BOX AND RETURNS TO THE BENCH.

SOL. GEN.	(TO THE JUDGE) With your permission, my Lord, I would like to ask a few questions of the young lady seated over there - Miss Manette - without that young lady having to enter the witness box. It is mostly a matter of identification, my Lord.
JUDGE	Proceed, Mr Solicitor General.
SOL. GEN.	Thank you, my Lord. (TO LUCIE) Miss Manette - look upon the prisoner. Have you ever seen him before?
LUCIE	Yes, sir. He was aboard the packet just described to you by Mr Lorry.
SOL. GEN.	Are you the young lady of whom the previous witness spoke?
LUCIE	I am.
SOL. GEN.	Did you have any conversation with the prisoner during the journey across the sea?
LUCIE	Yes, sir.
SOL. GEN.	Repeat it, please, Miss Manette.
LUCIE	He noticed that my father was much fatigued and in a weak state of health. He showed me how to shelter my father from the wind and weather. He was most kind.
SOL. GEN.	Had he come aboard alone?
LUCIE	No. There were two French gentlemen with him.
SOL. GEN.	Did they confer together?
LUCIE	Yes, sir.
SOL. GEN.	(HOLDING UP SOME PAPERS) Were papers like these handed about among them?
LUCIE	I could not be sure, sir.
SOL. GEN.	What was the prisoner's conversation, Miss Manette?
LUCIE	He told me that he was travelling on personal business of a delicate nature which might get people into trouble and so he was travelling under an assumed name. He told me that the business might continue to take him backwards and forwards across the Channel for a long time to come.
SOL. GEN.	Thank you, Miss Manette, that is all. You may sit down.
JUDGE	Do you wish to question the young lady, Mr Stryver?
STRYVER	No thank you, my Lord. No questions.
SOL. GEN.	(TO THE JUDGE) A few questions to this young lady's father, my Lord - if I may be permitted.
JUDGE	Proceed, Mr Solicitor General.
SOL. GEN.	(TO MANETTE) Doctor Manette, have you ever seen the prisoner before?
MANETTE	Once - when he called at my lodgings in London some three and a half years ago.
SOL. GEN.	Can you identify him as your fellow passenger on board that packet?
MANETTE	No, sir - I cannot.

19

SOL. GEN.	And why is that, Doctor Manette?
MANETTE	Because my mind is a complete blank concerning that time. It had been my misfortune to undergo a very long imprisonment, without trial, in France and I had only just been released from that imprisonment.
SOL. GEN.	Very well, Doctor Manette, that is, all - unless my learned friend who appears for the prisoner ...
STRYVER	No questions, thank you, Doctor Manette.
SOL. GEN.	The Crown now calls Thomas Kemp.
USHER	Thomas Kemp. Call Thomas Kemp.

KEMP GOES INTO THE WITNESS BOX.

SOL. GEN.	Now, Mr Kemp, I understand that you are employed as a waiter in a hotel in a certain garrison town, the name of which it is not expedient to reveal for reasons of security. Are you so employed?
KEMP	Yes, sir.
SOL. GEN.	Now, Mr Kemp, I ask you to look at the prisoner very carefully and tell me if you have seen him before.
KEMP	Yes, sir. In the coffee room of the hotel. It was some years ago but I remember him well.
SOL. GEN.	Did you ever see the prisoner on any other occasion?
KEMP	Not to my knowledge, sir.
SOL. GEN.	But you are quite certain that it was the prisoner who you saw in the hotel?
KEMP	Quite certain, sir.
SOL. GEN.	Thank you, Mr Kemp. No more questions.
KEMP	Thank you, sir.
JUDGE	Do you wish to question this witness, Mr Stryver?
STRYVER	No, thank you, my Lord. I have no ... (STOPS SPEAKING AS SYDNEY CARTON, WHO HAS APPEARED TO BE DISINTERESTED THROUGHOUT, PLUCKS HIS SLEEVE) One moment, my Lord. I beg your indulgence. I wish to confer with my learned friend, Mr Carton. (THEY WHISPER TOGETHER) Thank you, my Lord. Just one or two brief questions, if I may.
JUDGE	(CONSULTING HIS WATCH) Very well, Mr Stryver, but make sure they are brief.
STRYVER	I will, my Lord. (TO KEMP) Now, Mr Kemp, you have told the Court that you are quite certain that it was the prisoner you saw in the coffee shop of the hotel that day.
KEMP	Yes, sir.
STRYVER	And so you could not be mistaken. Now, look upon this gentleman, my learned friend. (INDICATES CARTON) Now look upon the prisoner. How say you? Are they not very much alike? With your Lordship's indulgence, I will ask my learned friend, Mr Carton to remove his wig.

WITHOUT WAITING FOR PERMISSION, CARTON REMOVES HIS WIG.

JUDGE	Mr Stryver - do you intend to try Mr Carton for treason?

STRYVER	No, my Lord. I merely wish to ask the witness whether he would have been so certain of identifying the prisoner as the man in the coffee room all those years ago - had he seen this illustration earlier. Well, Mr Kemp, would you?
KEMP	Well - no, I suppose not, sir. No, I wouldn't, sir.
STRYVER	Thank you, Mr Kemp. No further questions.

ALL IN THE COURT FREEZE EXCEPT JARVIS AND JERRY. JARVIS RUSHES ACROSS THE JERRY.

JARVIS	Jerry, Jerry - I want you take this paper which tells of the verdict, back to Tellson's Bank as fast as you can. I want you to take good care of it. (HANDS THE PAPER TO JERRY) Have you got it?
JERRY	Oh, yes, sir - I've got it all right. It's safe with me - wery, wery safe. Acquitted! Not Guilty! I'll get this back to the bank quicker than a flash of lightning. (RUSHES OFF)

THE COURT OFFICIALS AND THE PUBLIC CLEAR. DARNAY MOVES DOWNSTAGE AND IS SURROUNDED BY MANETTE, JARVIS, LUCIE AND STRYVER.

JARVIS	May I be the first to offer my congraulations, Mr Darnay? I hope that you have been preserved for a prosperous and happy life.
DARNAY	If I have been, then it must be due, in part, to the evidence you gave the court today. How can I thank you in sufficient measure?
JARVIS	It was nothing - nothing.
DARNAY	(TO MANETTE) And you, sir - I am obligated to you in a similar manner. (TO LUCIE) And to you also, Miss Manette. I will be forever in your debt. (TO STRYVER) Mr Stryver - what can I say? I will be under an obligation to you for the rest of my life.
STRYVER	It was an infamous prosecution, grossly infamous, but none the less likely to succeed on that account. It was obvious to me, that it was trumped-up charge contrived by that pair of despicable spies, Barsad and Cly. We must be grateful that the Court concurred. I have done my best for you, Mr Darnay, and my best is as good as another man's I believe.
JARVIS	Much better.
STRYVER	Well, you have been present all day and should know.

CARTON, WHO HAS BEEN STANDING APART FROM THE GROUP, SMILES WRYLY.

LUCIE	Shall we go home, my father?
MANETTE	Yes, we will go. Goodnight, Mr Darnay. I rejoice for you. Perhaps you would do us the honour of calling at our home in Soho one day. You would be most welcome.
DARNAY	Thank you, sir. I would be delighted to do so. Goodnight, sir, and God bless you.

ALL EXIT EXCEPT DARNAY AND CARTON WHO MOVES TO DARNAY

CARTON   Well, Mr Darnay?

DARNAY   I, also, have to thank you, Mr Carton.

CARTON   Why ever should you wish to do that? However, if you want to show your gratitude, then why the devil don't you dine with me tonight? I fear my own company this evening. Let me show you the nearest tavern where you may dine well.

DARNAY   I would be delighted to accompany you.

CARTON   (LINKING HIS ARM IN DARNAY'S) Come then - we go down Ludgate Hill to Fleet Street and from there ... (EXIT)

ACT ONE

Scene Six

THE DINING ROOM OF A TAVERN. LATER THE SAME EVENING. DARNAY HAS JUST FINISHED HIS MEAL. CARTON IS DRINKING PORT WINE.

DARNAY   That was ·an excellent. meal. You should have partaken of the splendid fare.

CARTON   I come here often but never to eat. (AFTER A PAUSE) It was an incredible chance that threw us together today, wasn't it?

DARNAY   Indeed, yes. But, quite frankly, Mr Carton, I hardly seem to be of this world yet.

CARTON   I'm not surprised. It is only a few hours since you were pretty far advanced on your way to the next. As for me, my greatest desire is to forget that I belong to this world. It has very little of good in it for me - apart from this port wine. So, we are not very much alike in that respect, are we, Mr Darnay?

DARNAY   No. Apart from an uncanny resemblance in features.

CARTON   Now, my dear Darnay, shall we drink a toast?

DARNAY   A toast? To whom?

CARTON   Why, to Miss Manette, of course. She was the admiration of the whole court.

DARNAY   Very well - to Miss Manette. (THEY DRINK)

CARTON   There's a fair young lady, eh? It is worth being tried for your life to be the object of her sympathy, eh?

DARNAY   Mr Carton, I would like to thank you most sincerely for the part you played in saving my life today.

CARTON   I did very little, Mr Darnay, and I have no idea why I did it. Now, tell me something, my dear Darnay. Do you think I like you?

DARNAY   Like me? I don't understand.

CARTON   It's quite a simple question - do you think that I like you? Well, do you?

DARNAY   You act as though you do but I'm not really sure that you mean it.

22

CARTON	That could be so.
DARNAY	(RISING) And now, if you'll excuse me, I am feeling very tired.
CARTON	Of course. On your way out, tell the waiter to bring me another bottle of port wine and to wake me at ten o'clock.
DARNAY	If that is what you wish. Ten o'clock, you say?
CARTON	Yes. I have to go to work tonight.
DARNAY	To work? For what purpose, may I ask?
CARTON	There are at least two cases to prepare for Stryver for tomorrow.
DARNAY	For Stryver? You prepare his cases for him?
CARTON	Oh, yes. Even when I was at Shrewsbury School, I did exercises for other boys and seldom did my own.
DARNAY	Why ever not?
CARTON	God knows - it was my way, I suppose. It was, and always has been a lame way summoning no energy and no purpose. Don't forget to order the wine, my dear Darnay.
DARNAY	I won't forget. Goodnight, Mr Carton.
CARTON	Wait! Just before you go - tell me, am I drunk?
DARNAY	I think that you have drunk too much, Mr Carton.
CARTON	Think? You know I have. Shall I tell you why, Mr Darnay? I am a disappointed drudge. I care for no man on earth and no man cares for me.
DARNAY	I find that to be a matter for much regret, Mr Carton. You might have used your undoubted talents to greater effect.
CARTON	Maybe, maybe. But don't let your own sober face deceive you, Mr Darnay. You never know what it might come to one day. A bottle of port and a call at ten o'clock, if you please. Goodnight, Mr Darnay.
DARNAY	Goodnight, Mr Carton and, once more - thank you. (EXIT)

VOICE OF THE NARRATOR

Sadly, sadly the sun set that night. It set upon no sadder sight than the man of good abilities and good emotions, incapable of their directed exercise, incapable of his own help and his own happiness, sensible of the blight on him, and resigning himself to let it eat him away.

ACT ONE
Scene Seven

THE WINE SHOP IN PARIS. A FEW WEEKS LATER. MADAME DEFARGE IS SEATED BEHIND THE BAR, KNITTING. DEFARGE IS SERVING A DRINK TO A MAN AT ONE OF THE TABLES. THE REST OF THE SHOP IS DESERTED. AN EXCITED MOB IS HEARD OFF, FOLLOWED BY THE SOUND OF A CARRIAGE BEING BROUGHT TO AN ABRUPT HALT. THERE IS A SCREAM FOLLOWED BY LOUD CRIES FROM THE CROWD. DEFARGE RUSHES TO THE DOOR. MADAME DEFARGE REMAINS UNMOVED AND UNMOVING.

CUSTOMER What is it? What's happened?

23

DEFARGE	(IN THE DOORWAY) It is a child. The coach of the Marquis has knocked down a child.
CUSTOMER	(NOW AT DOORWAY) Who is the child? Can you see?
DEFARGE	It's Gaspard's boy. He's bringing him in here.

GASPARD ENTERS CARRYING THE BODY OF A CHILD.

GASPARD	My child is dead! My boy has been killed!
DEFARGE	Lay him down over there. (INDICATES LEFT) We will send for a doctor.
GASPARD	(NOT MOVING) The child is dead, I tell you.

BY NOW THERE IS A CROWD OF PEOPLE IN THE ENTRANCE TO THE SHOP. TWO WOMEN ENTER AND GENTLY TAKE THE CHILD FROM GASPARD AND LAY HIM DOWN LEFT AND KNEEL BESIDE HIM. GASPARD STANDS LOOKING DAZED. THEN THE MARQUIS PUSHES HIS WAY THROUGH THE CROWD.

MARQUIS	Out of my way, you rabble. Do you not know who I am? I am the Marquis de St Evremonde - make way. (NOW INSIDE THE SHOP) It is extraordinary to me that you people cannot take care of yourselves and your children. One or other of you is forever in my way. How do I know what injury you may have caused to my horses? Here, take this. (THROWS A COIN)
GASPARD	My child is dead.
DEFARGE	Be brave, Gaspard. It is better for the poor little thing to die so, than to live in these times. At least he died in a moment without pain. Could it have lived an hour as happily?
MARQUIS	You are a philospher, eh? How do they call you?
DEFARGE	They call me Defarge.
MARQUIS	Of what trade?
DEFARGE	Vendor of wine, Monsieur the Marquis.
MARQUIS	(THROWING ANOTHER COIN) Pick that up, philospher and vendor of wine, and spend it as you will. (TO THE DOORWAY AND CALLING) The horses, are they injured?
VOICE	(OFF) They are unharmed, Monsieur the Marquis. We can continue our journey, if it so please you.
MARQUIS	(TURNING AT DOORWAY) It is indeed fortunate for all of you that no harm has come to the horses. (TURNS TO EXIT)

DEFARGE PICKS UP THE COIN AND THROWS IT AT THE MARQUIS. IT HITS HIM IN THE BACK.

MARQUIS	(SPINNING ROUND) Who threw that? Answer me! (SILENCE) You dogs! I would willingly ride over any of you and exterminate you from the earth. Out of my way! Let me pass, you vermin! (EXIT)

THE CROWD IN THE SHOP REMAIN SILENT. THE CARRIAGE IS HEARD DRIVING OFF.

DEFARGE	(TO THE CROWD) Gaspard - where is he? Did anyone see him leave?
WOMAN	Here was here a minute or two ago. He was standing over there by the door.
MAN	He looked as though he had been stunned.
JACQUES 1	(RUSHING INTO THE SHOP) Monsieur Defarge! Where is Monsieur Defarge?
DEFARGE	What is it, Jacques? What has happened?
JACQUES	It is Gaspard, the father of that dead child. I saw him climb under the carriage of the Marquis. He was swinging by the chain of the shoe when the carriage drove off. I called to him but I don't know if he heard me.
MADAME D.	(CHUCKLING) Under the carriage of the Marquis, was he? Well, Monsieur the Marquis, I trust that you will sleep soundly in your bed tonight! (LAUGHS AND THE OTHERS JOIN IN)

ACT ONE

Scene Eight

A ROOM IN THE CHATEAU OF THE MARQUIS -- LATER THE SAME DAY. DARNAY ENTERS FOLLOWED BY SELBY, A SERVANT.

SELBY	If you would wait in here, monsieur, I will tell your uncle that you have arrived.
DARNAY	Thank you, Selby.
SELBY	Monsieur - Before I tell Monsieur the Marquis, would you be able to spare a moment to speak to Monsieur Gabelle, the agent of the estate? He says that it is most urgent.
DARNAY	Of course, of course. Tell him to come in.
SELBY	Thank you, monsieur. (GOES TO DOOR AND CALLS IN A WHISPER) Monsieur Gabelle - Monsieur Charles will see you now. (TO DARNAY) Please ask Monsieur Gabelle to let me know when you wish me to advise your uncle that you have arrived. (SHOWS GABELLE IN AND EXIT)
DARNAY	How are you, Monsieur Gabelle? How are the peasants on this estate?
GABELLE	As well as can be expected, monsieur.
DARNAY	I trust that you are honouring your promise to me. I wish you to write to me at once, should there be even the slightest persecution of any peasant on this estate. I travel here as often as I can but, in between those visits, it is imperative that I am informed of any change in the situation.
GABELLE	I am frightened, monsieur.
DARNAY	Frightened? Of what, Gabelle?
GABELLE	There is much talk of an uprising, monsieur. And should that occur, I fear that, as agent of the estate, I might be be considered to be an enemy of the peasants. Take me back to England with you, monsieur, I implore you.

25

DARNAY	No, Gabelle. I could not do that, I'm very sorry. But you have my solemn promise that no harm will come to you. I swear that. Do you understand?
GABELLE	Yes, monsieur - thank you.
DARNAY	Now you had better leave before my uncle discovers that I have been talking to you. Advise Selby that my uncle can be informed of my arrival.
GABELLE	Very well, monsieur - and thank you.
DARNAY	Fear not, Gabelle. I will honour my promise, you may be certain of that.
GABELLE	God bless you, monsieur. (EXIT)

AFTER HE HAS GONE,   DARNAY WANDERS ABOUT THE ROOM AND THEN GOES TO LOOK OUT OF THE WINDOW.

MARQUIS	(AS HE ENTERS) Are - there you are, my boy. Can I offer you a drink?
DARNAY	No, thank you, Uncle. You left Paris this morning?
MARQUIS	This morning. And you, Charles?
DARNAY	I came direct from London.
MARQUIS	Ah. Well, my boy, what have you to tell me? You have not been to see us for some time.
DARNAY	I pursue the same object that took me away from France, Uncle. In fact, since I was here last, it has carried me almost to the brink of death. But it is a sacred object.
MARQUIS	Really?
DARNAY	But, had you know of my peril, I doubt if you would have lifted one finger to save me. Indeed, for all I know, you might have worked against me without my knowing it.
MARQUIS	(LIGHTLY) No, no, no!
DARNAY	Be that as it may, I know that if you so wished, your diplomacy would stop me and you would have no scruples whatsoever as to the means.
MARQUIS	I told you that long ago. Do you remember?
DARNAY	Oh, yes, I remember, Uncle. I believe that it is only the fact that you are out of favour at Court that has prevented me from being sent to some fortress for an indefinite period.
MARQUIS	(COLDLY) That is possible, my boy - quite possible. For the honour of the family, I could even resolve to incommode you to that extent but, as you so rightly say, I am at a disadvantage at present.
DARNAY	We have so asserted our station and authority in the past that I am certain that our name is detested more than any other name in France.
MARQUIS	Let us hope so. Detestation of the high is the involuntary homage of the low.
DARNAY	Monsieur, we have done wrong and we are reaping the harvest of our wrong.
MARQUIS	(WITH A SMILE) We have done wrong? Do tell me, my dear nephew, who has done wrong?

DARNAY	Our family whose honour means so much to both of us, in such different ways. Even in my father's time we injured every human creature who came between us and our pleasure.
MARQUIS	I will die perpetuating the system under which I have lived. But you, Monsieur Charles - you are lost.
DARNAY	This property and France are lost to me because I renounce them.
MARQUIS	Are they yours to renounce? France, perhaps, but is the property? Certainly it is not for as long as I remain alive.
DARNAY	I find myself bound to a system that is frightful to me. I am responsible for it, but powerless in it. In renouncing my future title, I am seeking to execute the last request made to me by my dear mother.
MARQUIS	Indeed? And what was that dying request?
DARNAY	She implored me to have mercy and to make amends for all the suffering our family has caused. That is the reason why I return to France so frequently in order that I may be certain that my promise to look after the peasants is, in fact, being honoured.
MARQUIS	That is both insolent and absurd. Repression is the only lasting philosophy. The dark deference of fear and slavery will keep the dogs obedient to the whip as long as this roof shuts out the sky.
DARNAY	Nevertheless, were this property to pass to me tomorrow, I would abandon it and live elsewhere. It is a wilderness of misery and ruin.
MARQUIS	Where do you intend to live under your new philosophy?
DARNAY	In England. It is my refuge.
MARQUIS	Do you know a compatriot who has also found refuge there - a doctor? He has a daughter.
DARNAY	I do.
MARQUIS	I thought you might. But now, my boy, we are both fatigued from travelling. (RINGS HANDBELL) I look forward to the pleasure of your company in the morning.

SELBY ENTERS.

MARQUIS	Light Monsieur my nephew to his chamber, Selby.
SELBY	(TO DARNAY) If you would follow me, monsieur.
DARNAY	Goodnight, Uncle.
MARQUIS	Goodnight, Nephew. Good repose.
DARNAY	And you, Uncle. (EXIT WITH SELBY)
MARQUIS	He can burn in his bed for all I care. Renounce the title and property indeed! (POURS A BRANDY)

GASPARD ENTERS AND MOVES SILENTLY TO THE MARQUIS.

MARQUIS	(RISING) Who is it? (SEES GASPARD) What do you want?
GASPARD	Your life for that of my child! (STABS MARQUIS WHO SLUMPS TO THE FLOOR) What was it you shouted as the carriage moved off, Jacques? 'Drive him fast to his tomb!'

ACT ONE

Scene Nine

DOCTOR MANETTE'S HOUSE IN SOHO. A YEAR LATER. DOCTOR MANETTE IS SEATED, READING. DARNAY ENTERS.

MANETTE   Charles Darnay! I rejoice to see you. We have been expecting you back for three or four days now. Sydney Carton was here yesterday and remarked that it was about the time you were to return.

DARNAY   I am obliged to him for his interest. And Miss Manette ...?

MANETTE   Is well and your return will delight us all. She is out on some domestic matter but should be back very soon.

DARNAY   Doctor Manette, I must confess to you that I knew that Miss Manette was not at home. I wanted to take the opportunity to speak to you on your own.

MANETTE   Then I suggest that you bring a chair over here by me and speak on.

DARNAY   (BRINGING A CHAIR) Thank you, sir. (SITS) Well, Doctor Manette, I have been most fortunate that you have allowed me to spend so much time here and for so long. It must be ever since I took up the appointment of French tutor here in England and ... and ...

MANETTE   Do go on, Mr Darnay.

DARNAY   Well, I do hope that the topic I am about to touch upon will not ...

MANETTE   Is Lucie the topic?

DARNAY   She is, she is. Dear Doctor Manette, I love your daughter dearly. If ever there was love in this world, I love her.

MANETTE   Have you spoken to her of your love?

DARNAY   No. Nor written.

MANETTE   (PRESSING DARNAY'S HAND) Thank you.

DARNAY   Heaven is my witness that I love her.

MANETTE   I have thought it might be so for some time now.

DARNAY   Doctor Manette, I want only to share your lives. I would be faithful until death. I do not wish to take from you your beloved companion and friend. Indeed, I hope that I might succeed in binding you even closer, were that possible.

MANETTE   Have you any reason to believe that Lucie loves you?

DARNAY   As yet, none. Doctor Manette, may I beg a promise from you?

MANETTE   Tell me what it is.

DARNAY   If, at any time, Miss Manette should confide in you in the manner I have just done, would you bear testament to what I have just said?

MANETTE   If she should ever tell me that you are essential to her perfect happiness, I will do so.

DARNAY   I thank you, Doctor Manette, with all my heart. I owe you so much that I must now tell you the truth.

28

MANETTE	The truth? About what?
DARNAY	About myself. My present name, although but slightly changed from that of my mother, as you may remember, is not my own. I want to tell you what it is and why I have to live in England.
MANETTE	Not now. Not now. If the day should ever come when Lucie confides in me that she loves you as you love her, then you can tell me on your wedding morning. Will you promise that?
DARNAY	Most willingly.
MANETTE	Give me your hand. She will be home before long. It might be better if she doesn't see us alone together tonight.
DARNAY	I understand.
MANETTE	Now go - and God bless you.
DARNAY	Thank you, Doctor Manette. I am indeed a happy man this day. Goodnight.
MANETTE	Goodnight, Charles.

EXIT DARNAY.

ACT ONE

Scene Ten

THE SAME. AN EVENING IN AUGUST. LUCIE IS SEATED. CARTON ENTERS.

LUCIE	Mr Carton! Do, please come in. My father is resting from the heat. Would you like me to call him?
CARTON	Oh, no. I just happened to be passing and, on a whim, decided to pay my respects.
LUCIE	And are most welcome, Mr Carton. Please come and sit down.

CARTON SITS ON A CHAIR CLOSE TO LUCIE.

LUCIE	(AFTER HE HAS SAT) Forgive me for saying so, Mr Carton, but you don't look at all well. Is there something the matter?
CARTON	The life I live is hardly conducive to health, Miss Manette.
LUCIE	Then, forgive me, is it not a pity to live such a life?
CARTON	It is indeed.
LUCIE	Then, why not change it, Mr Carton?
CARTON	It is far too late for that. I can never get better - only worse. (COVERS HIS EYES) Your pardon, Miss Manette. I am upset because I am aware of the importance of that which I have to say. It was no whim that brought me here today. There is something I have to tell you. Will you listen to me?
LUCIE	If it will make you happier, I will listen gladly.
CARTON	I am like one who died young. All my life might have been.
LUCIE	Do not say that, Mr Carton. It is not true.

29

CARTON	But it is, Miss Manette. Indeed it is.
LUCIE	But the best part of your life may still be to come. I am sure that you may be much, much worthier of yourself.
CARTON	If it had been possible that you could have returned the love of the man you see before you - self-destroyed, wasted, drunken creature of misuse, as you know him to be - he would have been conscious, in spite of his happiness, that he would bring you to misery. He would know, only too well, that he would disgrace you and pull you down with him. I know that you have no tenderness for me. I ask for none. I am even thankful that it cannot be.
LUCIE	Even without it, can I not save you? Can I not persuade you to alter course? Is there nothing I can do for you?
CARTON	(SHAKING HIS HEAD) Nothing, dear Miss Manette - nothing. If you will bear with me for a little longer, all you could ever do for me will have been done. I wish you to know that you have been the last dream of my soul. In my degredation, I have not been so degraded but that the sight of you with your father, and of this home made such a home by you, has stirred old shadows that I thought had died out of me long ago. I have even had ideas of trying to begin a new life and fighting off my present habits. But it was all a dream - a dream that ends in nothing. But I want you to know that it was you that inspired it.
LUCIE	Will nothing of it remain? Oh, Mr Carton, think again! Try again!
CARTON	No, Miss Manette. All through that dream, I knew, in my heart, that I was quite undeserving.
LUCIE	Then, since it is my misfortune to have more you more unhappy that you were before you knew me ...
CARTON	Please don't say that. If anybody could have saved me, you might have done.
LUCIE	Is it really too late? Have I no power for good with you at all?
CARTON	The utmost good that I am capable of now, Miss Manette. Let me carry through the rest of my misdirected life, the remembrance that I opened my heart to you. But I see that I distress you. I am almost finished. One final plea. Will you promise to share my secret with no one?
LUCIE	Your secret is safe with me, Mr Carton.
CARTON	(RISING) Thank you, Miss Manette. God bless you. (KISSES HER HAND AND MOVES AWAY? I promise you that I will never refer to this conversation again. (TURNING) But, before I go, I want you to know that for you and for any dear to you, I would do anything - anything at all. I would make any sacrifice. Try to hold me in your mind, at some quiet times, as ardent and sincere in this one thing. I would give my life to keep a life you love beside you. And now - farewell and a last God bless you. (EXIT)

30

ACT ONE

Scene Eleven

JERRY CRUNCHER'S LODGINGS. LATER THE SAME YEAR. MRS CRUNCHER IS KNEELING, LEFT, PRAYING. JERRY ENTERS AND CROSSES TO MRS CRUNCHER.

JERRY   Why - you're at it again and afore my wery face, you are.

MRS C.   I'm saying nothing, I'm not.

JERRY   Well then - don't! And don't meditate neither. You might just as well flop as meditate. You may as well go agin me one way as another. I reckons as how it was that there praying of yours as caused my wentures to go wrong tonight.

MRS C.   I don't know what you're on about, Jerry Cruncher.

JERRY   Of course you don't know, you stupid woman. How could you know when I hasn't told you yet? I've been frustrated in my trade, I have.

MRS C.   At the bank, do you mean?

JERRY   No - not at the bank. That's not my real trade, that isn't, as you wery well know. And stop cutting in with your stupid questions, woman. As I was about to say, I was sitting on my stool outside the bank when I sees this crowd approaching. Bawling and hissing, they was, round a hearse and one of them mourning coaches. There was only one man in the coach and the crowd was shouting at him. "Yah! Spy!" and such things - some of which was of too delikite a nature to repeat in front of a lady. And so, I asks one of them as was shouting, who was in the coffin. "It's that there Roger Cly," one of 'em says.

MRS C.   Who's he? I ain't never heard tell of any Roger Cly.

JERRY   Old Bailey spy, that's who he was. I saw him at that trial I went to when that Frenchman got off for treason. Anyhow, the crowd must have found out who he was for they set about this mourning coach. They pulled the bloke out and would have mobbed him but he escaped and rushed down a side street, shedding his coat, his hat and his mourning band as he went. The crowd soon made short work of them clothes. Tore 'em to bits, they did. Good job for him he wasn't inside 'em. Then, it came to me all of a sudden who he was. He was that other bloke at the trial. Bust me if I can think of his name - Buzzard or something like that. Anyhow, no sooner had he gone than this crowd crammed themselves into that mourning coach. There was at least eight inside and even more on top. As to the hearse, it's a wonder that poor old horse could drag it to the cemetery, there was that many on top and clinging to the sides. Anyway, in that manner, we escorted the coffin to its last resting place.

MRS C.   We? Did I hear you say we, Jerry Cruncher?

JERRY	I was most careful to conceal myself in a corner seat not facing the bank. And so we progressed to the cemetery. While we was on our way, I said to myself, I said, "Jerry Cruncher," I says, "you saw Cly with your own eyes at that there trial. He was a youngish sort of bloke and a straight one too." Now, being an honest tradesman - what some folks calls a resurrection man, I tells myself that his body is far too good to waste as food for the worms.
MRS C.	Jerry, Cruncher, you didn't go and ...?
JERRY	You was to honour and obey me, remember? Why don't you do it then?
MRS C.	I try to be a good wife, Jerry.
JERRY	Is it being a good wife to oppose your husband's trade? Is it obeying your husband to disobey him on the wital subject of his business?
MRS C.	I wish you had never taken up that dreadful business.
JERRY	And was you praying that agin me tonight, eh? Cos, if you was, you've really gone and done it this time, you have. If you're a religious woman, then God send me a heathen one, that's what I say. Oh, it went wrong all right, it did. I waited around that there cemetery for hours, I did for it to get dark and then it took best part of an hour for me and my partner to get that coffin out of the ground. And when we did, what do you think was in it? Roger Cly? No sign of him. All that was in that there coffin was a pile of broken paving stones. I reckons as how that there Cly had flown off somewhere to start again under another name now that he'd been discovered for what he was - a spy and an accomplice of that other spy. (SUDDENLY) Barsad!
MRS C.	What was that you said, Jerry Cruncher?
JERRY	Barsad - that's what I said. He was the other spy at the funeral - the one who ran away. I wouldn't be at all surprised if it wasn't him what arranged that mock funeral. He wanted Cly out of the way, I expect, in case he was discovered himself - he being in league with Cly. He's a nasty piece of work, that Barsad, if ever I saw one, wery nasty indeed. I tells you, Mrs Cruncher, you can flop down and pray against that Barsad any time you like, any time at all.

ACT ONE

Scene Twelve

THE WINE SHOP IN PARIS. A FEW WEEKS LATER. MADAME DEFARGE IS IN HER USUAL PLACE. CUSTOMERS ARE SEATED AT THE TABLES, PLAYING CARDS AND DOMINOES. DEFARGE ENTERS FOLLOWED BY A ROADMENDER. DEFARGE GOES TO THE COUNTER.

MADAME D. So, you have returned, my husband.

DEFARGE   Yes. I travelled with a roadmender who we will call Jacques.
           I met him as I was coming out of the city. He is a good
           man. Give me some wine for him. Give me the best we
           have.

A MAN GETS UP AND GOES OUT.

DEFARGE   (TAKING THE WINE) Here - sit down and drink this wine,
           Jacques. It's the best we have at present. (TO CENTRE
           TABLE) Jacques One, come and meet Jacques. He has
           something to tell you.

JACQUES ONE GETS UP AND GOES TO THE TABLE OF THE ROAD-
MENDER.   ANOTHER MAN GETS UP AND GOES OUT.

DEFARGE   This is Jacques One. We will call you Jacques Five. Now,
           tell your story.

ROADMAN   It must be almost a year ago - I was leaving my work
           on the road as the sun was setting when I saw the carriage
           of the Marquis de St Evremonde coming up the hill and
           there, clinging to the underside, was a man. The coach
           drove through the gates of the chateau with the man still
           underneath it.

JACQUES 1 What happened to him? Was he discovered?

ROADMAN   Not straightaway, but they scoured the countryside for
           months afterwards.

JACQUES 1 Afterwards? Why, what had he done?

ROADMAN   Why, he'd killed the Marquis, hadn't he?

JACQUES 1 Killed? The Marquis de St Evremonde?

ROADMAN   Didn't you know? Hasn't the news reached here yet?

THE NEWS IS PASSED ROUND IN EXCITED WHISPERS.

MADAME D. Just as I predicted, eh? (LAUGHS) The Marquis de St
           Evremonde is slain.

DEFARGE   Go on with your story.

ROADMAN   Some months later, I was working on the same stretch of
           road when I saw some soldiers coming over the brow of the
           hill with the man who had been under the coach. He had
           his hands tied to his sides. They pushed him and he fell
           over and they just laughed and picked him up. There was
           blood and mud all over his face. They took him to the
           prison in the village and left him there for days. You
           could see him staring out through the bars with his face
           still covered with mud and blood. Well, on Sunday, when
           the rest of the village was asleep, the soldiers and some
           workmen built a scaffold over the village well. They built
           it forty feet high. Then, they hanged him and left him
           hanging there forty feet above the ground. He may still
           be there now for all I know. I left at sunset and came
           straight here.

JACQUES 1 How say you of the rest of the Evremonde family?

MADAME D. To be registered as 'doomed for destruction'.

JACQUES 1	The chateau and all the race, eh?
MADAME D.	Yes. Extermination. (CACKLING) I will knit all the details into the register. (HOLDS UP HER KNITTING) All those registered for extermination are here. The details will always be as plain to me as the sun - never fear.
DEFARGE	(TO ROADMENDER) Come, Jacques Five, you must be tired after your journey. Come with me and I'll find you somewhere to lay your head. (THEY EXIT)
JACQUES 1	So - Gaspard has rid the world of the Marquis de St Evremonde. Excellent work - excellent! (CHUCKLES)

THE CROWD ARE EXCITED AND THERE IS A GENERAL BUZZ OF CONVERSATION. THEN DEFARGE RETURNS. HE BECKONS JACQUES ONE TO JOIN HIM AT THE BAR WITH MADAME DEFARGE.

DEFARGE	(IN A CONFIDENTIAL MANNER) What did Jacques of the police tell you while I was in the city?
JACQUES 1	There has been another spy commissioned to our Quarter.
MADAME D.	We must register him. What is his name?
JACQUES 1	He is English. He is called John Barsad. B-A-R-S-A-D.
MADAME D.	His appearance- is it known?
JACQUES 1	About forty years old - about five foot nine - dark hair and complexion - rather sinister looking.
MADAME D.	Good, good! I will register him.
JACQUES 1	Excellent, excellent! (CHUCKLES) And now, goodnight, madame, monsieur. (EXIT CHUCKLING)
MADAME D.	(AFTER JACQUES ONE HAS LEFT) Is something the matter, Husband?
DEFARGE	I am just tired, that is all.
MADAME D.	But you are depressed as well, aren't you? Why is that?
DEFARGE	It is such a long time coming.
MADAME D.	Revenge and retribution require a long time. It is the rule.
DEFARGE	You know, Wife, it is possible that it may not happen during our lifetime. We may not live to see the triumph.
MADAME D.	That is possible. But we shall have helped to bring it about. Nothing we have done has been done in vain.
DEFARGE	As you say - nothing we have done has been done in vain. Now, I will see if our new friend is settling down all right. (EXIT)

BARSAD ENTERS. MADAME DEFARGE PICKS UP A ROSE FROM THE BAR AND PINS IT TO HER HEADSCARF. ONE BY ONE, THE CUSTOMERS LEAVE.

BARSAD	(AT THE BAR) Good day, Madame. Have the goodness to pour me a small glass of your very best cognac.
MADAME D.	Certainly, monsieur. (SHE POURS THE DRINK AND THEN HANDS HIM THE GLASS IN SILENCE)
BARSAD	Thank you, madame. Your very good health. (TASTES THE COGNAC) Marvellous cognac, madame.

MADAME DEFARGE SMILES - SHE KNOWS IT IS NOT.

BARSAD   You knit with great skill, madame.
MADAME D.   I have been knitting for a long time, monsieur.
BARSAD   May I ask what it is for?
MADAME D.   A shroud, monsieur.
BARSAD   For use?
MADAME D.   Who knows? I may find a use for it one day.

TWO MEN ENTER - SEE THE ROSE AND LEAVE.

BARSAD   (LOOKING ROUND THE SHOP) Business seems bad.
MADAME D.   Very bad. The people are so poor.
BARSAD   Yes - poor, miserable people. So oppressed too, as you say.
MADAME D.   As you say, monsieur.
BARSAD   You think so too, of course.
MADAME D.   My husband and I are kept too busy in the shop to think.
BARSAD   I understand that news has only just reached here of the
              death of poor Gaspard. There will be much sympathy and
              anger in these parts when the news is passed round.
MADAME D.   Will there, monsieur?

DEFARGE ENTERS.

BARSAD   I was just saying to your wife that there may be much
              anger and sympathy here when they learn about Gaspard.
DEFARGE   I know nothing of it, monsieur.
BARSAD   I see. Tell me, when Doctor Manette was released, was it
              not you, his old servant, who had charge of him here?
DEFARGE   That is so, monsieur.
BARSAD   Did you know that his daughter is to be married? But
              not to an Englishman but to one who, like herself, is
              French by birth.
DEFARGE   No, monsieur. I did not know that.
BARSAD   And what an amazing coincidence it is. She is to marry
              the nephew of the Marquis for whose death poor Gaspard
              was raised to such exalted heights. This nephew, due
              to Gaspard's efforts, is now, himself, the Marquis de
              St Evremonde. But he lives in England and is no Marquis
              there. He calls himself Charles Darnay. (PAYS WITH
              A COIN) Now, I will wish you goodnight. I have so enjoyed
              our little chat. I will call again soon. Goodnight. (EXIT)
DEFARGE   If it is true that Miss Manette is to marry an Evremonde
              and we live to see the triumph, I hope - for her sake -
              destiny will keep her husband out of France.
MADAME D.   Her husband's destiny will take him to wherever he is to
              go and will lead him to whatever end it has in store
              for him. But we shall be waiting. (TAKES THE ROSE
              FROM HER HEADSCARF) We shall be waiting, never fear.

                        END OF ACT ONE

                             35

ACT TWO

Scene One

THE GARDEN OF DOCTOR MANETTE'S HOUSE. LATER THAT YEAR. DOCTOR MANETTE AND LUCIE ARE SEATED, SIDE BY SIDE, UNDER A TREE.

MANETTE   See, the moon is rising. By the time it rises again, you will ·be married.

LUCIE   Yes. Oh, I am so deeply happy that Heaven has so blessed my love for Charles, and his love for me. (LAYS HER HEAD ON MANETTE'S SHOULDER) Tell me, this last time, that you feel quite sure that no new affections of mine and no new duties of mine, will ever come between us.

MANETTE   Quite sure, my darling. My future is brighter, seen through your marriage, than it could ever have been without it.

LUCIE   If I had never met Charles, I should have been entirely happy with you.

MANETTE   If it had not been Charles it would have been another. Or if there had been no other, I should have been the cause and then the dark side of my life would have cast its shadow beyond myself and would have fallen on you. (AFTER A PAUSE) I have looked at that moon from my prison window when it has been torture to me to think of her shining upon what I have lost, and I have beaten my head against my prison walls. I have speculated thousands of times upon the unborn child from whom I had been torn away. Was it a son who would, one day, avenge his father? Perhaps it would be a daughter. I have pictured her, to myself, coming to my cell, and leading me out into the freedom beyond the fortress. I have seen her image in the moonlight often, as I now see you, except that I never held her in my arms.

LUCIE   Oh, my dear, my dear. Will you bless me as fervently tomorrow?

MANETTE   Lucie, I love you better than words can tell, and I thank God for my great happiness. My thoughts, when they were at their wildest, never rose near the happiness that I have known with you and that we have before us. (TAKES HER INTO HIS ARMS) I commend you to Heaven and humbly thank Heaven for having bestowed you upon me.

LUCIE   Oh, my dear, dear father.

MANETTE   And now, I think that we must go indoors. . Tomorrow will soon dawn and with it even greater happiness. Charles will be coming here early tomorrow morning, before the wedding. He wishes to confide in me and I have promised that I will listen to him. Come on then, my dear child, Let us go in.

LUCIE   Very well, dear Father. (RISES AND EXIT WITH MANETTE)

ACT TWO

Scene Two

DOCTOR MANETTE'S HOUSE. THE FOLLOWING MORNING AND OVER A PERIOD OF YEARS, IN LONDON AND PARIS. JARVIS AND MISS PROSS ARE WAITING ANXIOUSLY BY A CLOSED DOOR.

MISS PROSS How much longer do you think Mr Darnay will be in that room with Doctor Manette? Have they forgotten that my Ladybird is to be married within the hour?

JARVIS We must be patient, Miss Pross.

MISS PROSS What are they doing in there, for Heaven's sake? Would it not have waited for another day?

JARVIS I understand that Mr Darnay is honouring a promise made to Doctor Manette long before the marriage was planned. Married! Little did I think when I brought the sweet child across the Channel that she would marry Mr Charles.

MISS PROSS How could you have known? They only met for the first time on that boat. (STARTS TO CRY)

JARVIS There is no need to cry, Miss Pross.

MISS PROSS (SNIFFING) I'm not crying. You are the one who is crying. There is no point in trying to deny it. I saw you with my own eyes.

JARVIS Maybe, maybe. You see, my Pross, this is an occasion that causes a bachelor to speculate on all that he has lost. Dear, dear, dear – to think that there might have been a Mrs Lorry any time during the past forty years.

MISS PROSS Nonsense! You were a bachelor in your cradle.

JARVIS I suppose that you might ...

THE DOOR OPENS AND DARNAY AND DOCTOR MANETTE ENTER. DOCTOR MANETTE LOOKS DAZED AND UNHAPPY.

MANETTE Miss Pross, be so good as to tell Lucie that the moment has arrived. Mr Lorry, is the carriage waiting for us below?

JARVIS It is, dear Doctor Manette - it awaits you and Miss Lucie.

MANETTE Come then, let us waste no further time.

THEY ALL EXIT. AFTER A SHORT PAUSE, JARVIS AND MISS PROSS RE-ENTER. MISS PROSS WEARS A SHAWL AND JARVIS A DIFFERENT JACKET.

JARVIS I wish I knew what it was that passed between the good doctor and Mr Darnay before the wedding. It has had a profound effect on the doctor. It is many a long year since I have seen him so agitated.

MISS PROSS It was on the tip of my tongue to ask him what was troubling him, as soon as we returned from the church, but he went straight into that room and shut the door. What can we do, Mr Lorry?

JARVIS Very little, I fear. I think that we will have to wait and see what transpires. It might be a matter of ...

37

THE DOOR OPENS AND DOCTOR MANETTE STANDS IN THE DOORWAY WITH A SHOE IN HIS HAND. HE HAS REMOVED HIS COAT AND WAISTCOAT AND HIS SHIRT IS OPEN AT THE NECK.

MANETTE A young lady's walking shoe. It should have been finished long ago.

MISS PROSS Oh, my - what is to be done?

JARVIS Doctor Manette, look at me. You know me, my dear friend. Now, think again. This is not your proper occupation, is it?

MANETTE I must finish this shoe. The young lady is to be married tomorrow. (EXIT)

MISS PROSS Oh, me - all is lost.

JARVIS No, no - not all. However, we must make absolutely sure that this is kept a secret from all who know him and that, above all, Lucie is not informed. We will give out that the doctor is not well and requires a few days of complete rest. I will make arrangements to absent myself from the bank and remain here to look after him.

MISS PROSS That would appear to be a most excellent scheme, Mr Lorry. Might I suggest that we attempt to take him out for a walk each day?

JARVIS That would be splendid, providing that we can persuade him to come with us.

MISS PROSS I will share the vigil with you. We must divide the night into watches and observe him, at intervals from this room.

THEY SIT FOR A FEW SECONDS AND THEN RISE. THEY MOVE TO ANOTHER PART OF THE ROOM. MISS PROSS DISCARDS HER SHAWL.

MISS PROSS Nine days - nine days since he lost his memory. How much longer can we go on like this, Mr Lorry?

JARVIS I think that we are making some progress. In the past three days, he has put down his tools and come with us on our walk.

MISS PROSS But, as soon as we return, he goes straight back in there and continues with his shoemaking.

JARVIS I wish I knew what took place in that room on the wedding morning. Whatever it was, it was a great shock to Doctor Manette. I fear that it may take some time to ...

MANETTE (ENTERING FULLY DRESSED) My dear Miss Pross, Mr Lorry - is it not time for our walk?

MISS PROSS Have I been dreaming?

MANETTE Dreaming, Miss Pross? I don't understand.

JARVIS My dear Doctor Manette - what Miss Pross means is that you have not been in the best of health for the past few days and she was startled to see you so fully recovered.

MANETTE That is most kind. I appreciate your concern.

MISS PROSS (TRYING TO HIDE A TEAR) If you will pardon me, I will try to organise breakfast.

MANETTE Breakfast! What an excellent idea.

38

EXIT MISS PROSS.

JARVIS	Well, my dear friend, now that you are feeling so much better, I am most anxious to have your professional opinion on a most curious case which concerns a particularly dear friend of mine. I would be most grateful if you advise me on the matter - not only for my friend's sake but for that of his daughter.
MANETTE	What is the nature of the illness?
JARVIS	It is an old and prolonged shock.
MANETTE	How long did it last?
JARVIS	Nine days and nine nights.
MANETTE	How did it show itself?
JARVIS	In the resumption of an old pursuit.
MANETTE	Before this occurred, did you ever see him engaged in that pursuit?
JARVIS	Yes - once.
MANETTE	And the daughter of whom you spoke - does she know of this relapse?
JARVIS	It is known only to me and to a trustworthy friend.
MANETTE	That was very kind - most thoughtful.
JARVIS	Is there danger of another relapse?
MANETTE	I think it probable that the possibilty of this relapse was known and dreaded by him.
JARVIS	Would he remember what took place during that relapse?
MANETTE	Very little - walks in the park, perhaps, but only in the barest outline.
JARVIS	And the future?
MANETTE	I should hope that the worst is over.
JARVIS	The tools required to carry out that old pursuit - perhaps he should dispose of them.
MANETTE	They are old companions.
JARVIS	All the same, I would recommend to him that he sacrifices them - for his daughter's sake.
MANETTE	You ask a great deal of him, my friend ... but ... in his daughter's name, then, let it be done. But do not take them away when he is present. Let him miss his old companions after an absence. (AFTER A PAUSE) Now, we must look to the future. Lucie and Charles will be back here in a few days, will they not? Ah, I believe I smell breakfast. Shall we go in?
JARVIS	With the greatest of pleasure, Doctor Manette - with the greatest of pleasure. (EXIT)

AFTER A MOMENT OR TWO, ENTER MISS PROSS, DOCTOR MANETTE, JARVIS, LUCIE, DARNAY AND CARTON. THEY FORM INTO SMALL GROUPS.

CARTON	(APPROACHING LUCIE AND DARNAY) I have come to offer my congratulations to you both. I hope that you will be very happy.

LUCIE	Thank you, Mr Carton.
DARNAY	Thank you. That is most kind. You are the first person to call.
CARTON	Mr Darnay - I wish that we might be friends.
DARNAY	But we are already friends, I hope.
CARTON	Do you remember when you dined at the tavern after the trial? I was insufferable then about liking you and not liking you. I wish you would forget it.
DARNAY	I forgot it long ago. I had far more important things to remember about that day - how you helped to save my life and ...
CARTON	That? It was mere claptrap. I don't think that I cared what happened to you when I uttered it.
DARNAY	I refuse to believe that, Mr Carton.
CARTON	What I want to ask you is this - could you both put up with such a worthless fellow coming and going, at odd times, as a privileged friend? I doubt if I should abuse the permission. In all probability, I would only avail myself of it three or four times a year. It would satisfy me just to know that I had that permission.
DARNAY	You did not need to ask.
LUCIE	Of course you may.
CARTON	Thank you - thank you. And now I must go. Goodnight to both of you. (EXIT)
LUCIE	(TO DARNAY) Be generous with him always, my dear, and very understanding of his faults. I am sure that he has a heart that he very seldom reveals and that there are deep wounds in that heart. I know - I have seen it bleed. I am certain that he is capable of good things, gentle things - even magnanimous things. Think how strong we are in our happiness, and how weak he is in his misery.
DARNAY	I will always remember. God bless you, Lucie, in your sweet compassion.

LUCIE AND DARNAY MOVE TO ANOTHER PART OF THE ROOM AND SIT. THE OTHERS EXIT. LUCIE PLACES A SHAWL AROUND HER SHOULDERS AND PICKS UP SOME NEEDLEWORK. DARNAY PICKS UP A BOOK AND STARTS TO READ.

LUCIE	(AFTER A PAUSE) Have you ever seen a child so excited as our dear one was today?
DARNAY	(LOOKING UP FROM HIS BOOK) I'm sure that you were just as excited on your sixth birthday.
LUCIE	She was so tired that her little head had hardly touched the pillow before she fell asleep.

ENTER JARVIS.

DARNAY	My dear Mr Lorry, welcome. Come and sit down. You look exhausted
JARVIS	I am, I am. (CROSSING AND SITTING)
DARNAY	Why is that, my dear Mr Lorry?

JARVIS	We have been so busy that I haven't known what to do first. There is such uncertainty in Paris that the bank has had a run of confidence such as I have never seen before. Our customers over in Paris, don't seem to be able to confide their property to us fast enough. There is a perfect mania for sending it to England.
DARNAY	I don't like the sound of that. It has an ominous feel.
JARVIS	I agree - but we are not quite sure why it has happened so suddenly.
DARNAY	But you know how gloomy and threatening the sky is in France.
JARVIS	Indeed yes. Where is Manette?
MANETTE	(AS HE ENTERS) Here he is.
JARVIS	Good, good. I am pleased that you are at home. I have been surrounded by worries and forebodings all day long. They have made me nervous. I need your company to put me on an even keel again.
MANETTE	Then stay here and play backgammon with me.
JARVIS	Thank you, dear friend - I would like that very much. Prepare the board. But I must warn you I am not fit to be pitted against you tonight.

MANETTE FETCHES THE BOARD AND THEY SIT ONE EACH SIDE OF THE TABLE. LUCIE AND DARNAY REMAIN SEATED.

MANETTE	(AFTER THEY HAVE SHAKEN THE DICE) Your move then, my friend.

THEY CONTINUE TO PLAY THROUGHOUT THE FOLLOWING SCENE WITHOUT SEEING IT OR REACTING TO IT.

DEFARGE ENTERS DOWN LEFT FOLLOWED BY A CROWD OF MEN AND WOMEN.

DEFARGE	(CALLING) Keep near to me, Jacques Three. Jacques One and Jacques Two, separate and put yourselves at the head of as many patriots as you can muster. Where is my wife?
MADAME D.	Here - I am here, Husband.
DEFARGE	What is your plan?
MADAME D.	You will see me at the head of the women before long.
DEFARGE	Come then, patriots and friends, we are ready! To the Bastille! To the Bastille!
CROWD	The Bastille! The Bastille!
MADAME D.	To me, women! To me! We can kill as well as the men, when the Bastille is taken!
WOMEN	Kill! Kill! To the Bastille! Kill! Kill!

THEY ALL RUSH OFF RIGHT.

JARVIS	Is the precious child in bed after her birthday celebrations?
LUCIE	Yes, and sleeping soundly.
JARVIS	That's right - all safe and well - all safe and well.

41

LUCIE	Yes.
JARVIS	But I fancied that I heard distant rumblings from across the Channel.

A MOB RUSHES ON FROM THE LEFT.

CROWD	The prisoners! Release the prisoners! Get the records! Get the instruments of torture! Release the prisoners!

THEY RUSH OFF RIGHT.

DEFARGE ENTERS FOLLOWED BY A TURNKEY.

DEFARGE	Take me to the North Tower and be quick!
TURNKEY	All the prisoners have been released.
DEFARGE	Show me to One Hundred and Five North Tower and hurry!
TURNKEY	Come along then - this way.

THEY MOVE TO CENTRE STAGE

DEFARGE	Is this the cell?
TURNKEY	This is it.
DEFARGE	Pass your torch slowly along the walls. (TURNKEY DOES SO) Stop! What is that written there?
TURNKEY	It looks like the letters A and M.
DEFARGE	Alexandre Manette. Now, hold the light higher. (SEARCHES THE WALL) Ah, this is what I was looking for. (PUTS A PAPER INTO HIS POCKET) Now, for the Governor of the Bastille. His hour has come. Before the clock on the tower strikes again, his head will be parted from his body, I swear. Come! Come!
MADAME D.	(AS SHE ENTERS RIGHT) Husband! Husband! Come at once. They have captured old Foulon.
DEFARGE	Foulon?
MADAME D.	You remember Foulon - the one who told us that we should eat grass when we were famished.

THE CROWD ENTERS.

MADAME D.	They've found old Foulon hiding in the country. They've caught him and brought him here. They've bound him with ropes and tied a bunch of grass on his back. I think we should make him eat grass, don't you?
CROWD	Yes, make him eat grass! See how he likes eating grass!
MADAME D.	Come on, then. Every one of you pull up two handfuls of grass and we will stuff it all down his throat until he chokes. Then we'll cut off his head.
CROWD	That's right - cut off his head after his meal etc.
MADAME D.	Then go to the country and burn down the chateaux.
CROWD	Burn down he chateaux! We'll burn down the chateaux!
MADAME D.	Tell them to start with the chateau of the Evremondes.
CROWD	(RUSHING OFF) Let's go and feed old Foulon! Cut off his head! Let's burn down the chateaux! etc. etc.
DEFARGE	At last it has come, my wife - at last it has come!

42

MADAME D.	Almost, my husband - almost. (THE DEFARGES EXIT)
MANETTE	(TO JARVIS WHO IS SITTING STARING INTO SPACE WITH A BACKGAMMON PIECE IN HIS HAND) My dear friend, my dear friend - you appear to be miles away. It is your move now, I think.
JARVIS	Yes, Doctor Manette, you are right. It is indeed.

ACT TWO

Scene Three

JARVIS'S OFFICE IN TELLSON'S BANK. THREE MONTHS LATER. JARVIS IS SEATED, DARNAY IS LEANING ON THE DESK.

DARNAY	My dear Mr Lorry, please forgive me but I must say it - I think you are too ...
JARVIS	Old?
DARNAY	A long journey in unsettled weather and to a disorganised country and a city that may not be safe, even for you.
JARVIS	My dear Charles, it is safe enough for me. Nobody will interfere with an old fellow of my age. Moreover, it is imperative that I go to rescue a number of important documents before they are seized and destroyed.
DARNAY	I wish I was going too.
JARVIS	You, a Frenchman born?
DARNAY	It is because I am a Frenchman born that I feel I should go. Are you really going tonight?
JARVIS	I am.
DARNAY	Are you taking anybody with you?
JARVIS	I'm taking Jerry Cruncher. Nobody will suspect him of being anything other than a British bulldog.
DARNAY	I admire your gallantry and youthfulness.
JARVIS	Nonsense! Nonsense! Perhaps when I have executed this little mission, I might consider retiring and living at ease. Time enough, then, to think about growing old. Oh, there is one other matter. There's a letter here on my desk. I would imagine that it was sent to the bank in the hope that they might be able to forward it to the addressee. I have asked everybody in the bank and nobody has any idea of the present address of the gentleman to whom it is addressed. (HANDS HIM THE LETTER) Is it possible that you might know where to deliver it?
DARNAY	(LOOKING AT THE NAME ON THE LETTER) I will take charge of it.
JARVIS	You know where to deliver it?
DARNAY	I do. (MOVES AWAY AND READS THE LETTER) "Prison of the Abbaye - June 21st 1792. Monsieur heretofore the the Marquis. After having long been in danger of my life at the hands of the village, I have been seized, with great violence and indignity, My house has been destroyed. I have been brought to Paris and have been imprisoned here.

43

They tell me that the crime is treason because I have been employed by an emigrant. Will you not come to deliver me? For the love of Heaven, I beg you to do so and release me from this prison of horror. Your afflicted former employee, Gabelle." (STEPS BACK TO THE DESK) Mr Lorry, would you be so good as to take a verbal reply to this letter - for a very good friend?

JARVIS	Of course. Where is it to?
DARNAY	To a prisoner in the Abbaye. His name is Gabelle.
JARVIS	What is the message?
DARNAY	Simply that the letter has been read and he will come.
JARVIS	Any time mentioned?
DARNAY	He will start on his journey tomorrow night.
JARVIS	Shall I mention the name of this gentleman?
DARNAY	No, Mr Lorry - no name. Just say that he is coming. Gabelle will understand.

ACT TWO

Scene Four

A GUARD ROOM IN PARIS. TWO DAYS LATER. AN OFFICER IS SEATED AT A DESK. SOLDIERS, PATRIOTS ETC ARE ASLEEP AND AWAKE, DRUNK AND SOBER AND STANDING AND LYING ABOUT THE ROOM.

DEFARGE	(AS HE PUSHES DARNAY INTO THE ROOM) In here and hurry.
OFFICER	Citizen Defarge, is this the emigrant Evremonde?
DEFARGE	It is.
OFFICER	Your age, Evremonde?
DARNAY	Thirty-six.
OFFICER	Married?
DARNAY	Yes.
OFFICER	Where married?
DARNAY	In England.
OFFICER	Where is your wife now?
DARNAY	In England.
OFFICER	Very well, Evremonde - you are consigned to the prison of La Force.
DARNAY	Under what law and for what offence?
OFFICER	We have new laws, Evremonde, and new offences since you were here last.
DARNAY	Please - I beg you to understand that I have come here, of my own free will, as a direct response to that written appeal from a fellow countryman which lies on your desk. All I ask is that I may be given the opportunity to respond to that appeal without further delay. Surely that is my right, is it not?
OFFICER	(STOLIDLY) Emigrants have no right, Evremonde. (SANDS THE NOTE HE HAS BEEN WRITING AND HANDS IT TO DEFARGE) La Force - in secret.

44

DEFARGE   Come with me, Evremonde.

THEY MOVE AWAY LEFT AND CHECK.

DEFARGE   (IN A LOW VOICE) Was it you who married the daughter
           of Doctor Manette?
DARNAY   (SURPRISED) Yes it was. How did you know that?
DEFARGE   My name is Defarge and I keep a wine shop in the Quarter
           Saint Antoine. Possibly you have heard of me?
DARNAY   Indeed, yes. My wife came to your house to reclaim her
           father. Is that right?
DEFARGE   Yes, she did. In the name of that newly born, sharp female,
           La Guillotine, why ever did you come to France?
DARNAY   For the reason I told the officer a minute ago. Everything
           is changed here. I am lost. Will you render me a service?
DEFARGE   I cannot.
DARNAY   Then will you tell me - the prison I am going to, I'm
           not going to be buried there, am I, without any means
           of presenting my case?
DEFARGE   You will find out when you get there.
DARNAY   Monsieur Defarge - it is of the utmost importance that
           I get in touch with Mr Lorry of Tellson's Bank here in
           Paris. He must be told that I am going to be thrown
           into prison. Would you do that for me?
DEFARGE   (RATHER UNHAPPILY) I can do nothing for you. My
           duty is to my country. I am the sworn servant of my
           country against you. I will never do anything for you.
           Understand that. Now, come along with me. We have
           wasted enough time already.

ACT TWO

Scene Five

A ROOM IN TELLSON'S BANK IN PARIS. A FEW DAYS LATER.
JARVIS IS SEATED, WRITING.

JARVIS   (PUTTING DOWN HIS PEN AND LOOKING OUT FRONT)
           May God protect the innocent in this dreadful city tonight.
           There is danger in the air wherever you go. (STARTS
           TO WRITE AGAIN)

LUCIE AND DOCTOR MANETTE BURST INTO THE ROOM.

JARVIS   (RISING) Lucie! Doctor Manette! What are you doing here?
LUCIE   Oh, Mr Lorry, it is Charles.
JARVIS   What has happened to him?
LUCIE   He is here - in Paris. He has been here for two or three
           days. We had no idea that he was here. He came on an
           errand of mercy and was stopped at the barrier and sent
           to prison.
JARVIS   Prison? Oh, no, that is terrible.

A BELL RINGS OFFSTAGE·

MANETTE	(STARTLED) What is that? (MOVES TOWARDS WINDOW)
JARVIS	Don't look out of the window, dear friend, for your life's sake!
MANETTE	(TURNING, WITH A SMILE) You forget that I have a charmed life here in Paris - indeed in all of France. I have been a prisoner in the Bastille. There is no patriot who would lay a finger on me. That is how we managed to get past the barrier and gain news of Charles.
JARVIS	What prison is he in?
LUCIE	La Force.
JARVIS	And the child - young Lucie - where is she?
LUCIE	With Miss Pross. They are waiting in some gardens across the street from here.
JARVIS	They must not stay there - they could be in great danger. You must bring them here at once.
LUCIE	Very well. I will go and fetch them now. (EXIT)

AFTER SHE HAS GONE, MANETTE GOES TO LOOK OUT OF THE WINDOW.

JARVIS	That grindstone out there in the courtyard is where the soldiers sharpen their swords. They are murdering the prisoners.
MANETTE	Dreadful! Dreadful!
JARVIS	Doctor Manette, as you have so much power here, you must make yourself known to those in charge and get them to take you to that prison. It may be too late but I beg you to go now - without further delay.
MANETTE	You are right. I must go now.
JARVIS	Good, good. God go with you.
MANETTE	Goodbye, dear friend, goodbye. Dreadful! Dreadful! (EXIT)

JARVIS GOES AND SITS AT HIS DESK. LUCIE AND MISS PROSS ENTER AND SIT. THEY FREEZE FOR A FEW SECONDS. THEN -

LUCIE	It is more than twenty-four hours since my father left to go to that prison and we have not heard a word.
JARVIS	Patience, dear heart, patience. You may be certain that your father will ... What is that noise on the stairs?

THE DEFARGES BURST INTO THE ROOM.

JARVIS	(RISING) Who are you? What do you want?
DEFARGE	Don't you remember me? You came to my wine shop in St Antoine.
JARVIS	Oh, yes - now I remember. Have you come from Doctor Manette?
DEFARGE	Yes. He sends you this note. (HANDS PAPER TO JARVIS)
JARVIS	(READING) "Charles is safe but I cannot leave here yet. The bearer has a short note from Charles. Let the bearer see Lucie."
DEFARGE	(HANDING A NOTE TO LUCIE) This is for you.
JARVIS	(WHILE LUCIE READS NOTE) You are Madame Defarge?

46

MADAME D. I am.

JARVIS Why have you come here?

MADAME D. To look at you all so that I will be able to recognise you if I need to. It is for your own safety.

LUCIE Charles begs me to have courage. He says that he is well and that my father's influence has helped a great deal. Then he asks me to kiss young Lucie for him. That is all. (TO DEFARGE) May I answer this?

DEFARGE No - no answer.

JARVIS Lucie, my dear, when you were reading that note from Charles, Madame Defarge was telling me that she has come here to see those she has the power to protect so that she can identify them if necessary.

MADAME D. Where is the child?

LUCIE Asleep in the next room.

MADAME D. Take me to her.

LUCIE You will not disturb her?

MADAME D. Just to see her - that is all I require.

LUCIE Very well. Please come with me. This way. (THEY EXIT)

JARVIS (TO DEFARGE) This is our very good friend Miss Pross. She has come to France very much against her will.

DEFARGE My wife has seen her. No doubt she has noted her.

MISS PROSS Noted me? And what does that mean, my good man?

JARVIS It only means that Madame Defarge will be able to recognise you again should the occasion arise.

MISS PROSS Very well - but I don't like it. I don't like it at all.

MADAME DEFARGE AND LUCIE RE-ENTER.

MADAME D. It is enough, Husband. I have seen them. We can go now.

LUCIE You will be good to my poor husband. You will do him no harm. Will you help me to see him if you can?

MADAME D. Your husband is not my business here. It is the daughter of your father who is my business now.

LUCIE For my sake then - for my child's sake - be merciful to my husband.

MADAME D. Did not your husband say, in that note, that your father has influence? Surely, that should help to release him. But you'll get no help from me.

LUCIE As a wife and mother, I implore you to have pity.

MADAME D. The wives and mothers we have been used to see, since we were as little as that child in there, have not been shown any consideration. We have known their husbands and fathers laid in prison and kept from them, often enough. All our lives we have seen our sisters suffer, in themselves and in their children. We have seen poverty, nakedness, hunger, thirst, sickness, misery, oppression and neglect. We have borne this for a long time. Is it likely that the trouble of one wife and mother would be much to us now? (TO DEFARGE) Come, Husband, our business here is concluded. Let us go. (EXIT)

47

ACT TWO

Scene Six

THE MANETTE'S LODGINGS IN PARIS. FIFTEEN MONTHS LATER.
JARVIS ENTERS.

LUCIE	Ah, dearest friend, is there any news?
JARVIS	Nothing further, my dear.
LUCIE	How much longer must we wait? Charles has been in that awful prison for fifteen months.
JARVIS	All we can do is to remain patient, my dear Lucie. Even your father has not succeeded in persuading them to bring him to trial. But we must be grateful that he is still in that cell and alive - unlike the poor devils who have been dragged out and massacred. At least, now that your father has been appointed prison doctor, he should be able to carry messages between Charles and yourself.
LUCIE	That would be wonderful.
JARVIS	A new era has been born in France now that the king is dead. They call it the Republic of Liberty, Equality, Fraternity and Death. That great black flag waves, day and night, from the towers of Notre Dame. They say that three hundred thousand men and women rose against the tyrants. It would seem that the Cross has been superseded by the guillotine.

MANETTE ENTERS.

JARVIS	Is there any news?
LUCIE	How is Charles? Is he ... still ...
MANETTE	Nothing can happen to him without my knowledge and I am certain that I can save him eventually. There is a small consolation I can offer you. There is an upper window in the prison to which Charles can sometimes gain access at three in the afternoon. It is possible that he might be able to see down into the street below. If you were to stand in a place I can show you, he should be able to see you, but I'm afraid you won't be able to see him.
LUCIE	Just show me the place and I will go there every day, no matter what the weather - every day until he is brought before the tribunal to prove his innocence.

ACT TWO

Scene Seven

THE TRIBUNAL IN PARIS. SEVERAL MONTHS LATER.   FIVE JUDGES
WEARING FEATHER HATS, PRESIDE. A JURY SITS ON BENCHES.
THE CROWD INCLUDES THE DEFARGES. DOCTOR MANETTE AND
LUCIE SIT ON A BENCH TOGETHER WITH JARVIS AND MISS PROSS.

USHER	Charles Evremonde, called Darnay!

48

CROWD   Take off his head! An enemy to the Republic! Curse all Evremondes! Show him Madame Guillotine! etc.

THE PRESIDENT RINGS HIS BELL FOR SILENCE.

PRESIDENT   Is it true, Evremonde, That you have lived many years in England?
DARNAY   It is.
PRESIDENT   In that case, are you not an emigrant?
DARNAY   I submit - not within the sense and spirit of the law.
PRESIDENT   Why not?
DARNAY   Because I have, of my own free will, ·relinquished a title and a station that were distasteful to me and left this country before the word emigrant in its present meaning, was in use. I left here to live by my own industry rather than be a burden to the oppressed people of France.
PRESIDENT   What proof have you of this?
DARNAY   I submit to the court the names on this paper. (HANDS PAPER TO USHER WHO PASSES IT TO THE PRESIDENT)
PRESIDENT   I understand that you married in England.
DARNAY   I did - but not to a Englishwoman.
PRESIDENT   To a citizen of France?
DARNAY   Yes - by birth.
PRESIDENT   Her name and family?
DARNAY   Lucie Manette - only daughter of Doctor Manette, the good physician who sits there.
CROWD   Doctor Manette! He was in the Bastille! For eighteen years! Long live Doctor Manette! etc.
PRESIDENT   (RINGING FOR SILENCE) Why did you return to France?
DARNAY   Because of the pressing entreaty of a French citizen who believed that his life was in danger because of my absence. I came back to try to save him by testifying on his behalf. Is that a crime in the eyes of the Republic?
CROWD   No! No! He came to save a French citizen! He risked his life! No crime! No crime! etc.
PRESIDENT   (RINGING HIS BELL) The name of that citizen?
DARNAY   He is my first witness. His name is Citizen Gabelle.
PRESIDENT   Let him appear before the tribunal.

GABELLE TAKES THE STAND.

PRESIDENT   This letter I have in front of me. Is this the letter you sent to the prisoner? (USHER SHOWS THE LETTER)
GABELLE   Yes it is. I sent it from the Abbaye where I was prisoner.
PRESIDENT   Are you no longer a prisoner there?
GABELLE   No. I was released three days ago.
PRESIDENT   Very well - that is all. You may go. The next witness - Doctor Manette.

MANETTE TAKES THE STAND AS GABELLE STEPS DOWN.

PRESIDENT   Doctor Manette - tell the court of your relationship with the prisoner.

MANETTE   He was my first friend on my release from the Bastille after eighteen years. He has remained in England, always faithful and devoted to my daughter to whom he is married. Indeed, far from being in favour of the aristocratic government there, he has actually been tried for his life as a foe of England and a friend of France. I would ask you to call Monsieur Lorry, an Englishman, who is here in this court, to confirm my story.

CROWD   Let him go! Let the prisoner go! He is a friend of the Republic! Release him! etc.

PRESIDENT   Foreman of the jury, do you wish to hear more?

FOREMAN   No more. We find the prisoner - not guilty.

CROWD   Not guilty! He's not guilty! etc.

PRESIDENT   I declare the prisoner, Charles Evremonde called Darnay, free to go.

THE CROWD GOES MAD, CHEERING AND SHOUTING. A WOODEN CHAIR IS PRODUCED, DRAPED WITH A FLAG. THEY HOIST DARNAY UP INTO THE CHAIR AND CARRY HIM AROUND THE STAGE AND THEN TO STAGE LEFT SHOUTING 'LET US TAKE HIM HOME IN TRIUMPH, HE IS A FRIEND OF THE REPUBLIC' ETC. WHEN THEY REACH STAGE LEFT, LUCIE IS WAITING. DARNAY IS PUT DOWN AND THEY EMBRACE.

MAN   Are we going back with an empty chair?

2nd MAN   No - let's put Estelle in the chair. She can be the goddess of liberty.

THEY PUT A GIRL IN THE CHAIR AND SHOUTING "LONG LIVE THE GODDESS OF LIBERTY." , THEY CARRY THE CHAIR ACROSS THE STAGE AND OFF RIGHT. WHILE THIS HAS BEEN GOING ON, THE COURT OFFICIALS HAVE REMAINED IN PLACE. ALL OF THE CROWD HAVE GONE APART FROM THE DEFARGES. THEY MOVE TO THE PRESIDENT AND SHOW HIM A PAPER WHICH HE READS.

LUCIE   Charles, Charles - let me thank God for sending you back to me.

DARNAY   Lucie, my own, I am safe at last. And now, dearest, speak to your father. No other man in the whole of France who could have done what he has done for me.

ALL THREE CONTINUE TO EMBRACE. WHILE THIS IS GOING ON, THE PRESIDENT CALLS TWO SOLDIERS AND SPEAKS TO THEM URGENTLY AND THEY HURRY OFF TO THE GROUP LEFT.

SOLDIER 1   The Citizen Evremonde called Darnay?

DARNAY   Who wants me?

SOLDIER 1   You are again a prisoner of the Republic.

DARNAY   But I have just been found not guilty and acquitted.

SOLDIER 1   You are summoned to appear before the Tribunal again.

MANETTE   One moment. Do you know who I am?

SOLDIER 1   Yes, Doctor Manette.

MANETTE   Then, tell me what this is all about.

50

SOLDIER 1	He has been denounced by the St Antoine Section.
MANETTE	Denounced for what?
SOLDIER	Don't ask me anything more, Citizen Doctor. If the Republic demands sacrifices of you, then, I am sure that, as a a good citizen, you would be prepared to make them, would you not?
MANETTE	Just tell me who denounced him?
SOLDIER 1	It is against the rules but, as it is you that asks, I will tell you. He is denounced by Citizen and Citizeness Defarge and one other.
DARNAY	What other?
SOLDIER 1	You will be answered shortly - that is all. Come, Evremonde, we are pressed for time.

LUCIE ALMOST FAINTS BUT IS SUPPORTED BY JARVIS AND DOCTOR MANETTE. FLANKED BY THE SOLDIERS, DARNAY WALKS BACK TO THE COURTROOM. THE CROWD RETURN AND TAKE THEIR PLACES. DARNAY IS PUT BACK INTO THE DOCK. JARVIS, LUCIE AND DOCTOR MANETTE SIT ON A BENCH TOGETHER. THE JUDGES CONFER SILENTLY.

CARTON ENTERS RIGHT ON THE FORESTAGE AND MEETS BARSAD WHO HAS ENTERED LEFT.

CARTON	I have been looking for you, Mr Barsad.
BARSAD	Looking for me? What are you doing in Paris?
CARTON	Making enquiries about a friend who was tried and acquitted but, I understand, has been re-arrested.
BARSAD	Your friend must be Charles Darnay.
CARTON	That is so. Now, I hope that Doctor Manette's name and influence will will stand him in good stead once more. But it may not be so. Now, Mr Barsad, these are desperate times when desperate games are played for desperate stakes. Now - the stake I have decided to play for is a certain acquaintance of mine in the Conciergerie where they house the condemned prisoners. That acquaintance I propose to win is a certain John Barsad.
BARSAD	You'll need to have good cards.
CARTON	I'll run over them, shall I? Let us see what I have got. Prison spy, emissary of Republican committees, now a turnkey, now a prisoner but always a spy and a secret informer. Represents himself to his present employers under a false name. Now, those are very good cards, don't you agree, Mr Barsad? I believe that he is still in the employ of the aristocratic English Government, and is the spy of Pitt. That's a card not to be beaten. Would you like me to play my ace - denunciation of this spy to the nearest Section Committee? Look at your own hand, Mr Barsad. Don't hurry. While you are doing so, can I mention a certain Roger Cly - a fellow patriot of yours, I believe?

BARSAD	He's dead – Roger Cly is dead. I put him in his coffin.
CARTON	But I have it, on the very best authority, that the coffin was full of paving stones. Don't you like your hand, Mr Barsad? Are you going to play?
BARSAD	I throw it in. What do you want?
CARTON	I understand that you are a turnkey at the Conciergerie and can choose when you want to be on duty.
BARSAD	Yes, that is so.
CARTON	Right. (TAKING BARSAD BY THE ARM AND LEADING HIM OFF) This is what I want you to do ...

THE TRIBUNAL RESUMES.

PRESIDENT	Charles Evremonde, called Darnay, released earlier this day, you now appear in front of this tribunal denounced as an enemy of the Republic – an aristocrat – one of a family of tyrants. I will ask the Prosecutor to tell the Court who denounced the prisoner.
PROS.	Three voices – Ernest Defarge and his wife, , Madame Defarge and Alexandre Manette.
CROWD	Doctor Manette! Doctor Manette denounced this one! He must be guilty if Doctor Manette denounced him! etc.
MANETTE	(RISING) President, I must protest. This is quite untrue. I have not accused the husband of my daughter. Why should I do such a thing?
PRESIDENT	Citizen Manette, be silent or you may put yourself outside the protection of the law.

DEFARGE GOES INTO THE WITNESS BOX.

PROS.	Tell the Court what you did when you were inside the Bastille.
DEFARGE	I knew that a certain prisoner had been confined in a cell known as one hundred and five, North Tower. I went to that cell and found this written paper in a hole in the chimney. It is in Doctor Manette's handwriting.
PRESIDENT	I now ask the Prosecutor to read that paper.
PROS.	"I, Alexandre Manette, write this in my cell in the Bastille in the year 1767. When I was a young physician, I was called to the chateau of the Marquis de St Evremonde to attend to a young peasant woman suffering from a brain fever. I discovered that this condition had been brought about by the behaviour of the brother of the Marquis. It seems that this brother desired this young woman and brought about the deaths of her husband, her brother and her father. The young woman died but I considered it my duty to report the affair to the Minister of Justice. Some short time after I had reported the matter, I was called again to see the Marquis. He had my report to the Minister. He burnt it in front of me and I was taken, without trial, to this cell in the Bastille. Now, I, Alexandre Manette, being in possession of my

52

	right mind, do, this day, denounce all the Evremondes and their descendants for all time."
CROWD	(SHOUTING) Save him now, Doctor! Kill him! Down with all the Evremondes! Down with tyrants! etc.
PRESIDENT	Foreman of the jury, what is your verdict?
FOREMAN	Guilty.
PRESIDENT	Charles Evremonde known as Darnay, you have been found guilty of being an enemy of the Republic and an oppressor of the poor. Death within forty-eight hours. Court adjourned.

EXIT PRESIDENT, COURT OFFICIALS AND SHOUTING CROWD.

LUCIE	(RUSHING TO DARNAY) May I embrace him - just once?
SOLDIER	Only a minute, then.
DARNAY	(TAKING LUCIE IN HIS ARMS) Farewell, beloved, farewell. We shall meet again where the weary are at rest.
DARNAY	(TO MANETTE) Dear, dear Doctor Manette, I know now how much you must have suffered when I told you my true name on my wedding morning. We thank you with all our hearts. Heaven be with you.

HE GOES OFF WITH THE SOLDIERS. THE FAMILY EXIT SLOWLY. THE DEFARGES COME DOWNSTAGE. CARTON RE-ENTERS AND STANDS LISTENING.

MADAME D.	That was a good day's work indeed. I look forward to seeing Evremonde again. (LAUGHS) It was an excellent start.
DEFARGE	What do you mean?
MADAME D.	We're not stopping while there are still Evremondes living.
DEFARGE	Where are you going to stop, then?
MADAME D.	At extermination.
DEFARGE	Generally, I would agree but the doctor has suffered greatly. Did you see his face when the paper was read in Court?
MADAME D.	I begin to wonder if his face may be the face of an enemy of the Republic.
DEFARGES	But, his daughter - what anguish she is suffering. Didn't you see her after the trial?
MADAME D.	I saw her today and I have seen her on other days. I have seen her in the street looking up at the prison cell. I have but to lift my finger and ...
DEFARGE	No - leave it at that - go no further.
MADAME D.	I have had the name of Evremonde on my register for years. They are doomed to extermination and destruction. I'll tell you something I've never told you before. That peasant family who were destroyed by the Evremondes - one was my sister's husband, one was my brother and the third was my father! Tell the wind and the fire where to stop - but don't tell me. Don't tell me!

THE DEFARGES EXIT.

CARTON HURRIES OFF RIGHT.

ACT TWO

Scene Eight

A ROOM IN TELLSON'S BANK IN PARIS. THE SAME DAY. JARVIS IS SEATED AT A DESK. CARTON ENTERS IN A GREAT HURRY.

CARTON   Mr Lorry, I have to speak to you on a matter of great importance. (PRODUCES A PAPER) This is a certificate which enables me to pass out of the city of Paris. See, it is made out in the name of Sydney Carton. I want you to keep it for me until tomorrow. I shall be seeing Charles and I don't think it would be wise to take that paper with me.

JARVIS   Seeing Charles? How will you be seeing him? He is in prison.

CARTON   That is where I will be seeing him.

JARVIS   But ...

CARTON   (PRESSING ON) Now, take this other certificate as well. It enables Doctor Manette and his daughter and her child to pass the barrier at any time. Miss Pross has a similar paper for herself and for Mr Cruncher. These passes are valid at present but they could be revoked at any time, and I have good reason to think that they might.

JARVIS   Are they in danger?

CARTON   They are in great danger of being denounced by that Defarge woman. I heard it from her own lips. Don't look so horrified. You can save them. You have money and can buy the means of transport to the coast by the quickest possible method. Now then - early tomorrow morning, have the horses ready so that they can start at two in the afternoon exactly. Can you do that?

JARVIS   It will be done, I promise you.

CARTON   Good. Now, tell Lucie, tonight, of the danger to herself and the child. Tell her that it is imperative that she leaves Paris with you at two o'clock tomorrow afternoon. Tell her that more depends upon it than she could possibly imagine. Have all the arrangements made in the courtyard here, including the taking of your own seat in the carriage. Now - and this is of vital importance - the moment that I come to you, take me into the carriage and drive away without question. Wait for nothing except to have my seat occupied and then set off for England. Arrange for Miss Pross and Mr Cruncher to follow in another lighter coach. They should be able to overtake us and lead the way to the coast. Now, Mr Lorry, will all this be done?

JARVIS   (GRASPING CARTON'S HAND) You have my solemn promise. But don't worry, it does not just depend upon an old man, for I shall have a young and ardent man by my side.

CARTON   By the help of Heaven you shall! Now, finally, I want you to promise me that nothing whatsoever will influence

	you to alter the course on which we now stand pledged to each other.
JARVIS	Nothing, Carton.
CARTON	Remember these words tomorrow - change the course, or delay it - for any reason - and no life can possibly be saved and many lives must be sacrificed.
JARVIS	I will remember them. I promise to do my part faithfully.
CARTON	And I hope to do mine. Now, goodbye, Mr Lorry. (EXIT)

ACT TWO

Scene Nine

A PRISON CELL. THE NEXT DAY. DARNAY IS SEATED, WRITING. HE THROWS DOWN HIS PEN AND STARTS TO PACE UP AND DOWN.

BARSAD	(OFF) He has never seen me here. I have kept out of his way. Go in alone. I'll wait here - and hurry!

THE DOOR OPENS AND CARTON ENTERS. DARNAY TURNS.

CARTON	Of all the people upon earth, you least expected to see me.
DARNAY	Are you a prisoner?
CARTON	No. By chance, I have power over one of the keepers here. That is how I managed to get in here. I come from your wife, my dear Darnay, with a most urgent message.
DARNAY	I don't understand.
CARTON	You don't need to understand. Just do as I ask. Now, quickly, change that coat for this one of mine.
DARNAY	You don't understand, there is no escaping from this place. I implore you not to add your death to mine.
CARTON	Have I asked you to pass that door? When I ask that, you can refuse. Now, I see that there is pen and ink on the table. Is your hand steady enough to write?
DARNAY	It was before you came in.
CARTON	Then steady it again and write down what I dictate to you. Quick, friend, quick!

DARNAY SITS AT THE TABLE AND PICKS UP THE PEN.

CARTON	Write exactly what I tell you.
DARNAY	To whom do I address it?
CARTON	To no one.
DARNAY	Do I date it?
CARTON	No - no date. Now, start writing. "If you remember the words that passed between us, long ago, you will understand this letter when you receive it. I know that you will remember them. It is not in your nature to forget them." (PUTS HIS HAND INTO HIS POCKET) "Forget them." have you written that?
DARNAY	Yes. What's that in your hand?
CARTON	You'll know very soon. Now, continue writing - only a few more words. "I am thankful that the time has come when I can prove those words. That I do so now is not

55

	a matter for grief or regret. (MOVES HIS HAND SLOWLY TOWARDS DARNAY'S FACE)
DARNAY	What's that vapour?
CARTON	What vapour? Start writing again, quickly!

AS DARNAY PICKS UP THE PEN, CARTON COVERS HIS FACE WITH A PAD. AFTER A SHORT STRUGGLE, DARNAY FAINTS. CARTON PUTS ON DARNAY'S COAT, PICKS UP THE LETTER AND PUTS IT INTO THE POCKET OF THE JACKET DARNAY IS WEARING. HE TIES HIS HAIR BACK AND GOES TO DOOR AND CALLS SOFTLY.

CARTON	Barsad! Come on in.

BARSAD ENTERS.

CARTON	You see - it wasn't very dangerous for you, was it?
BARSAD	Mr Carton, will you keep your side of the bargain?
CARTON	Mr Barsad, I will be true to the death.
BARSAD	You'd better go if that tally of fifty-two is to be correct.
CARTON	Don't worry. I shall soon be in no position to harm you and the others will be far from here, please God. Now, then, I pretended to be faint when I came in past the guards - and I'll be even fainter when you take me out. Take him to the courtyard by Tellson's Bank, as we arranged. Then, put him in the carriage yourself. Tell Mr Lorry to remember my words of last night and his sworn promise to drive away as fast as he can.
BARSAD	I will. Now, time is running out.
CARTON	I know it well. Take care of my friend and leave me now - at once.

CARTON HELPS BARSAD HALF-CARRY DARNAY TO THE DOOR.

BARSAD	(CALLING) Here - come and give me a hand with this one - he's fainted.

THE CELL DOOR IS OPENED AND A GAOLER HELPS BARSAD WITH DARNAY. THEY EXIT.

CARTON	(AFTER A PAUSE, MOVING UP TO THE DOOR TO LISTEN) Not a sound. No raised voices. They must be passing the guards by now. (PAUSE) Still no sound. (GOES QUICKLY ACROSS TO THE WINDOW AND, GRASPING THE BARS, STRAINS TO LOOK OUT - AFTER A PAUSE) Yes, there they are - they're out in the street. Now, if Barsad keeps his side of the bargain, Charles should be in the coach in less than five minutes. Then, if they get past the barrier without question, they'll be on their way to England and safety - please God. (GOES TO THE CHAIR AND SITS)

AFTER A PAUSE TO INDICATE THE PASSING OF TIME, THE CELL DOOR OPENS AND A GAOLER ENTERS.

GAOLER	Follow me, Evremonde.

CARTON FOLLOWS THE GAOLER ACROSS THE STAGE TO A KNOT
OF PRISONERS WHO HAVE JUST ENTERED.

GAOLER   Inside here, Evremonde - and quick about it. I've a lot
more to fetch. There's fifty-two on the list.

SEAMSTRESS (MOVING TO CARTON) Citizen Evremonde, I am a poor
little seamstress who was with you in La Force.

CARTON   (NOT TURNING TO HER) Yes - of course. What was
the charge?

SEAMSTRESS Being involved in plots against the Republic. But the
just Heaven knows that I am innocent. Who would think of
plotting with a poor little creature like me? But they would
not listen to me. But I am not afraid to die. May I ride
with you on the cart, Citizen Evremonde, and will you
hold my hand? It would give me courage.

CARTON   (TURNING TO HER) Of course you may.

SEAMSTRESS Thank you. (SEES CARTON - IN A WHISPER) But you
are not ...

CARTON   (TAKING HER FINGERS AND PLACING THEM OVER
HER LIPS) Hush! Hush!

SEAMSTRESS (IN A WHISPER) Are you dying for him?

CARTON   And his wife and child. Now, hush, hush!

SEAMSTRESS May I hold your hand, brave stranger?

CARTON   Yes, my poor sister - to the last.

GAOLER   (AS HE ENTERS WITH TWO MORE PRISONERS) Right -
that's enough for the first cart. Outside, you lot - and
quick about it.

THEY GO TO THE TUMBRIL THAT IS WAITING FOR THEM.

GAOLER   Come on - up you get. You've got a rendezvous, you have
- a rendezvous with a lady - Madame Guillotine (LAUGHS
LOUDLY)

THE PRISONERS GET UP ONTO THE TUMBRIL, CARTON AND THE
SEAMSTRESS LAST SO THAT THEY ARE AT THE REAR OF THE
TUMBRIL. IT MOVES OFF.

ACT TWO

Scene Ten

THE MANETTE'S LODGINGS IN PARIS. A FEW MINUTES LATER.
MISS PROSS ENTERS CARRYING A BOWL OF WATER. ALMOST AT
ONCE, MADAME DEFARGE ENTERS FROM THE OPPOSITE SIDE.
MISS PROSS SEES HER AND DROPS THE BOWL.

MADAME D. The wife of Evremonde - where is she?

MISS PROSS You might, from your appearance, be the wife of Lucifer
but you'll not get the better of me. I am an Englishwoman

MADAME D. I was on my way to the place where I have a reserved
seat and where they hold my knitting for me, when I
decided to call and pay my compliments to the wife of
Evremonde. Where is she? I want to see her.

MISS PROSS	You can stand there all day and ask that question but you'll get no reply from me.
MADAME D.	It'll do her no good to keep herself hidden from me. Go and tell her I wish to see her. Do you hear me?
MISS PROSS	How many more times must I tell you that I will not let you see her? You are a wicked woman and we want nothing to do with you. Now, go away.
MADAME D.	Don't talk to me like that, you imbecile. I demand to see her. Stand away from that door and let me go to her.
MISS PROSS	Now, you listen to me. I don't care an English twopence for myself, but I know that the longer I keep you here, the greater hope there is for my ladybird. If you so much as lay a finger on me, I'll pull out that black hair of yours by the handful.
MADAME D.	(TO THE DOORWAY) Citizen Doctor! Wife of Evremonde! Child of Evremonde! Any person but this miserable fool, answer the Citizeness Defarge!
MISS PROSS	You will not enter that room, do you hear?
MADAME D.	I don't think there is anybody in that room. If they have gone they will be pursued and brought back here.
MISS PROSS	But I shan't let you leave here to raise the alarm.
MADAME D.	I have been in the streets from the first. Nothing has ever stopped me yet and nothing ever will. I will tear you to pieces if you try to hold me. Now, out of my way, you imbecile pig!

MADAME DEFARGE ATTACKS MISS PROSS AND THEY STRUGGLE IN THE DOORWAY. THEN, THE STRUGGLE TAKES THEM THROUGH THE DOORWAY AND OUT OF SIGHT.

MISS PROSS	(OFF) Your pistol is under my arm. You shan't have it.

THERE IS THE SOUND OF A PISTOL SHOT AND THEN MISS PROSS STAGGERS BACK INTO THE ROOM.

MISS PROSS	Oh me! Oh me! She is dead. What is to be done? What will happen if they find the body and charge me with her murder? Come, woman - pull yourself together! (SHE STRAIGHTENS HER BONNET) There - that's better.

JERRY CRUNCHER ENTERS.

MISS PROSS	Oh, there you are, Mr Cruncher. What news?
JERRY	They are safely away. I watched the carriage drive off and I waited to see them clear the barrier. They are on their way to Calais and home. Thank God, that's what I say - thank God!
MISS PROSS	Mr Cruncher - .I asked you a question.n. Why are you speaking so quietly? I can't hear a word of what you are saying.
JERRY	(SHOUTING) I said they are away! They are safe!

58

MISS PROSS	I still can't hear you. And why is there no noise in the streets?
JERRY	No noise? Can't you hear the roll of them dreadful carts?
MISS PROSS	What was that you said?
JERRY	Come along, Miss Pross, come along. We've got to get into our coach and try to catch 'em up. I wouldn't mind too much about not hearing them dreadful carts so near to their journey's end. Hurry up, Miss Pross. There's no time to waste if we want to catch up with the others.

ACT TWO

Scene Eleven

AT THE GUILLOTINE. SHORTLY AFTERWARDS. THE TUMBRIL WITH THE PRISONERS ENTERS AND MOVES FROM RIGHT TO CENTRE. THE SQUARE IS LINED WITH SHOUTING, JEERING CITIZENS. ON EACH SIDE OF THE TUMBRIL ARE SOLDIERS WITH DRAWN SWORDS.

CROWD	To the guillotine! Down with aristocrats! How many today? Let's have the first one! etc.
MAN	(TO BARSAD) Which one is Evremonde?
BARSAD	There - at the back. The one holding the girl's hand.
MAN	(SHOUTING) Down with Evremonde! Cut off his head!
BARSAD	Hush!
MAN	What's the matter? Why shouldn't I shout at him?
BARSAD	He's going to pay the forfeit. It will all be over in less than five minutes. Let him be at peace.
MAN	Ugh! Down with Evremonde! Let's have his head!
WOMAN 1	Therese! Where's Therese Defarge? Has anybody seen her?
WOMAN 2	She's never missed yet.
WOMAN 1	And she won't miss this one, you can be sure Therese!
WOMAN 2	She'll have to hurry, then. Here's the first of 'em now.
WOMAN 3	And that Evremonde's among 'em and she's not here. Look - I've got her knitting and a place saved for her.

THE SOLDIERS START TO GET THE PRISONERS TO DISMOUNT FROM THE TUMBRIL. WHEN THEY ARE ALL DOWN, CARTON AND THE SEAMSTRESS STAND AT THE HEAD OF THE PRISONERS.

SEAMSTRESS	I think you were sent to me by Heaven.
CARTON	And you to me. Now, keep your eyes on me, my dear, and look at nothing else.
SEAMSTRESS	I don't mind anything as long as I can hold your hand. Will it be quick?
CARTON	Yes, it will be quick. Don't be afraid.
SEAMSTRESS	May I ask you one last question?
CARTON	Of course. What is it, my dear?
SEAMSTRESS	I have a cousin whom I love dearly. Do you think it will seem long to me while I wait for her in the better land?

CARTON   There is no time there and no pain.
SEAMSTRESS That is a great comfort to me. Am I to kiss you now? Has the moment arrived?
CARTON   Yes, my dear.

THEY KISS

CARTON   God bless you, my child.
SEAMSTRESS God bless you, dear, brave man.

SHE IS DRAGGED TO THE FOOT OF THE LADDER WHICH LEADS UP TO THE GUILLOTINE PLATFORM AS THE CROWD JEERS. WHEN SHE REACHES THE TOP OF THE LADDER, CARTON MOVES SLOWLY TO THE FOOT OF THE LADDER. HANDS STRECH DOWN TO PULL THE SEAMSTRESS ONTO THE PLATFORM. THEN, IN THAT POSITION, ALL FREEZE.

CARTON   It is a far, far better thing that I do than I have ever done. It is a far, far better rest that I go to than I have ever known.

VOICE OF THE NARRATOR

I am the Resurrection and the Life, saith the Lord; he that believeth in me, though he were dead, yet shall he live: and whosoever liveth and believeth in me shall never die.

ROLL OF DRUMS

CURTAIN